THE BEST IS YET TO COME

WHAT THE FUTURE HOLDS

Franklin D. Murdock

Thelma Reyna, Editor

VerveStar, LLC
Los Angeles – Houston

VerveStar, LLC
5405 Wilshire Blvd, Suite 268
Los Angeles, CA 90036
www.VerveStar.com
ISBN: 978-0-9828848-4-3

Book Layout ©2014 Navarone Books

Ordering Information:
Quantity sales. Special discounts are available on quantity purchases by corporations, associations, and others. For details, contact the "Special Sales Department" at the address above.

The Best is Yet to Come by Franklin D. Murdock. —1st ed.

THE BEST IS YET TO COME

WHAT THE FUTURE HOLDS

Franklin D. Murdock

The Best is Yet to Come

Acknowledgments

First and foremost, all my accolades are for the Holy Spirit of God who has formed and shaped me over the last forty years to be a committed servant of my Lord. I am especially humbled and grateful that God called me, then guided me, to study the Word more intently and to meditate on the concealed truths revealed to me. I can truly proclaim that after studying and writing this story, I am a deferent person. I know now what He means when He invites you to enter His rest and be at peace.

I want to acknowledge that along the way He has brought anointed teachers and pastors that have led me to the level of knowledge of God and Jesus that I have today. To name them all would take volumes; but a few have certainly earned special recognition. The greatest provider of the bread of life is a television broadcasting network which is dedicated to bringing the gospel of our Lord to all people of the world. A few of these evangelists that are most prominent in my mind are Dr. Fredric Price, Kenneth and Gloria Copeland, Adrian Rogers, John Hagee, Billy and Franklin Graham, Joyce Myer, Paula White, and, last but not least, Dr. Chuck Missler. These good people, along with Paul and Jan Crouch, have untiringly and unselfishly given of themselves to bring the good word of the gospel to every part of this world through television and have founded TBN, a 24/7 commercial-free all-Christian programming, broadcasting in many languages and covering every inhabited area on this planet via use of satellites.

There are many more people of God who deserve mention, but their good works are their reward, and I give them, collectively, my deepest gratitude and respect. They and their families manifest through their public display of life a witness to the loving kindness and grace of our God toward all mankind.

I cannot leave it there, for I must acknowledge the love expressed and received from the three wives God sent to be my help meets[1], and every member of their families who now call me Dad or Grandpa. I receive with humility this blessing, and I am forever grateful.

---

[1] There is a difference of word meaning as noted between this carnal world and God's Kingdom. Help *meet*, or help *mate*? In the Bible God states for Adam He formed His female man from a rib of Adam and gave it to him as his help *meet*. (Genesis 2:18, 20). The ancient Hebrew dictionary defines *meet* as a protector, surrounding and providing assistance when needed, and a helper. Verse 24 states: "Therefore shall a man leave his father and mother and cleave unto his wife: and they shall be one flesh." God uses the word *mate* only with beasts and birds in Isaiah 34:15-16, and the ancient Hebrew definition of the word *mate* is as a neighbor, a comrade, a brother, close friend, or a lover, and does not refer to one's spouse.

Preface

I write this book in obedience to a strong, urgent influence in my spirit for reasons of which I am not sure. At this critical time in God's age of the dispensation of Grace, all civilized people are apprehensive concerning the possibility that life in this world, as we know it today, is about to change. The unknown factor creates fear and apprehension. I am not going to even try predicting exactly how and when these changes will occur, but that they *will* occur is an absolute eventuality. God and Jesus provides ample descriptions of these changes, and They have made it unmistakably clear that we should be alert and prepared, ready to respond correctly as He has given instruction.

Within these pages is the revelation of the mystery of life. I am confident that there will be at least one reader who will repent from some unacceptable lifestyle and find the true and glorious rest and peace of God. I have written two previous books—*My Father's Wondrous Love* and *Blessing or Presumption*; but they were different from this present one, as they were based on events that had happened during my life. This book, on the other hand, is based on what God has *declared* is going to happen, and His enlightenment of the end of this age. I have reason to believe this final stage has already begun. However, I will begin this book with an accounting of an incident that truly happened to me, and as a result has led me into a more intimate and glorious fellowship with God and Jesus through His word.

I Peter 4:7 states: "The end of all things is at hand: be you therefore sober, and watch unto prayer."

I PRAY THAT THESE WORDS FIND YOU RECEPTIVE TO HIS BLESSING AND GRACE.

The Best is Yet to Come

Table of Contents

The Best is Yet to Come

CHAPTER 1

Introduction

It was 29 years ago. In July 1981, I experienced a life-changing visitation from God. It was the third visitation I had experienced, but it surpassed the others regarding the impact it had upon my life. The previous two visitations had concerned specific personal events in my life, and I had audibly heard God's voice and experienced an awesomely engulfing peace and rest being in His presence. The first visitation was during wartime in 1945, and the second was shortly before my first wife died in 1980. Both of these had been amazing, and I should have responded more positively; but I was too caught-up in the rudiments of this material world at those times to realize their true meaning and influence.

The Third, Most Important, Visitation

The third time, our Lord really got my attention, and I knew that this was different. It was less than one year after I was widowed the first time. Along with an older brother who was living with me, we were visiting family in Salt Lake City, and three older brothers and I decided to play a round of golf. On the third fairway my brother, who shared a golf cart with me, hooked his drive far out into high rough. We rode the cart through the rough to find his ball. I accidentally drove into and out of a hole dug in the ground by some rodent. The sudden bump was jarring to my body and drove my tail bone up into my spine. In excruciating pain, I had difficulty walking and was unable to finish the game.

I visited two chiropractors on two successive days, to no avail. Then my sister, who had experienced nerve damage from cancer surgery, took me to see her neurosurgeon, who admitted me into a hospital. Twice daily at that hospital, I was taken by gurney to a special area for physical therapy. The second day, while resting in my bed between therapy sessions, I experienced something that I had never felt before: an awesomely inexplicable, strangely captivating, yet hugely comforting feeling. It was a stirring of my spirit and hearing in my inner self, not through my ears but through my *being*. A voice was talking to me with great authority, and it had the same effect on me as my two earlier visitations, but this was more intense. I immediately grabbed pencil and paper to write what I was hearing in my spirit.

There were five distinct and different instructions or commandments, as follows:

1. I want you to find all you can about me. I want you to completely understand my character and nature, my will and purpose and master plan for man and earth.
2. I want you to find out all you can about Satan, his nature and character, for I want you to know your adversary, and be able to recognize his presence and actions when they affect you.
3. Find all you can about yourself. Why are you here and what is your destiny? Understand how much you know about me and Jesus.
4. Tell me what relationship you have with me and with Satan because you will have relationships with both of us as long as you live in today's world environment and in your mortal body, or until Satan is permanently annihilated from both earth and heaven's realm.
5. Find out what sin is. Not the fruits of sin, but the root of all sin.

I was stunned and bewildered. I had never before experienced such a profound and emotional message, one that definitely affected the re-orientation and purpose of my life. Surprisingly I suddenly had no discomfort in my back.

The next morning a nurse brought me a release form and asked me to sign it. I asked, "What is it for?" She replied that the doctor wanted to perform a mylogram on my spine. I refused to sign the form and told her I had been healed. That evening the doctor visited me, and after I told him of my experience, he said he was discharging me the next morning. When discharged, I returned to my brother's home, and the following day my three brothers and I played that interrupted golf game.

My Transformation: Learning and Following God's Word

My life has never been the same since this amazing encounter with my heavenly Father. Nothing spectacular happened immediately, and I did not suddenly begin talking in an unknown language or tongues. Life went on as usual, with me doing all that is normal in being firmly involved with the fundamentals of living a life in this material world. Some changes began occurring slowly but surely. Praise be to God, for He began molding and shaping me into a new creature.

I continue receiving almost daily revelations of knowledge and wisdom. I had to learn the new, full meaning of the word "love" as God would have me know it, and to think in a new manner on a higher plane. It required that I prioritize my daily time more thoughtfully and apply my efforts more intensely, with a greater focus on my work, seriously studying God's word. I found the teaching ministries broadcast on the Trinity Broadcast Network supremely helpful and encouraging in stimulating me as I diligently studied the word of God.

After I began applying myself to studying His intimate and personal letter to me, the Bible, I soon learned what diligence really means as it relates to believing, and trusting God without question or doubt and following His instructions. As I searched the scriptures for His revelations and guidance, and sought answers to my questions, I heard the voice of my Father speaking to me through His written word. I then understood what the apostle Paul penned in his letter to the Saints in Rome recorded in Romans 10:17, as follows: "Faith comes by hearing, and *'hearing by the word'* of God." I think it appropriate to point out, scientifically, that we hear by the oscillations of air against our eardrums; but hearing the word of God is in our heart.

In the gospel of John 10: 3, 4, 27, Jesus proclaims that His sheep hear and know his voice and will follow him. I became highly motivated to gain knowledge of God and my Lord Jesus.

The Rigors of Learning God's Word

I had to learn to study the word more attentively than I was accustomed to. I found that I had to read a scripture over and over many times, meditating each time, and for some scripture, this would consume many days. I submerged myself in His word, each time perceiving something more comprehensive than what I had understood the first time I read it. By doing this I receive precept upon precept.

Then I must listen intently for His promised guidance. I expectantly await the interpretation of His written word from His Holy Spirit, and not blindly accept, or seek, the counsel of man. Yet I must acknowledge that there are anointed teachers of the word, and when I have found them, I have been grateful for their enrichment of my learning and understanding. Two such individuals are Chuck and Nancy Missler, internationally recognized authors, speakers, and experts in the dissemination of God's word. I'll discuss their ministry in another part of this book.

God faithfully provides sustenance to our souls; but, as he has written, we cannot absorb this knowledge instantaneously. So God feeds us with loving tenderness no faster than we can absorb it. I give thanks to my Father, for I still have an intense burning desire to gain what the apostle Paul describes as the "Excellency of the knowledge of God's Christ, Jesus. For what He has done by the mystery of the cross for me, His praise will always be in my heart and on my lips."

In the gospel of John, addressing the promise of our eternity, Jesus Christ proclaimed the following: "Let not your heart be troubled, you believe in God, believe also in me. In My Father's house are many mansions; if it were not so, I would have told you. I go to prepare a place for you, and if I go and prepare a place for you, I will come again and receive you to myself; that where I am, there you may be also." This alludes not only to heaven, but here on earth during the thousand-year millennium, and then into the glorious utopian age of eternity to be with our Lord Jesus, and our heavenly father for everlasting. Remember, Jesus' promise to return for His church was given to bring them heavenly comfort.

How comforting to us, in this troublesome world, to know that Jesus will be back for all of us who have followed Him. For this reason, and that you, too, can know your adversary and be not easily deceived, I write to share with you God's revealed knowledge of things to come, and His promises relevant to this end time. For indeed, the best is yet to come!

The Best is Yet to Come

CHAPTER 2

Absolutes

In this chapter I take the liberty of using the adjective *absolute* as a noun, and specifically, as a *predicate noun*, whereby the latter is merely another name or synonym for the subject of the sentence. If I say, "Jack is my brother," the word "brother" is a predicate noun, referring back to the subject of the sentence, the noun "Jack." We can see that in constructions like these, the subject and predicate noun are one and the same. So "Jack" and "brother" are the same thing, the same person.

Consider the following statements, and note that the word *absolute* is merely another name or term for the subject or subjects of each sentence below.

1. God and Jesus are absolutes.
2. His word is an uncompromising absolute.
3. God's word is truth; truth is an absolute.[1]
4. God is Holy and cannot lie. That is an absolute.
5. The promises made by God, both those that are desirably attractive and those that are repugnant, are absolutes.
6. Prophesies including the end of the church age (the rapture) and first resurrection are absolutes.
7. The doom and destiny of Satan the God of all evil, master of deception, is an absolute. This will culminate the final purpose before initiating God's final preparation of His designed plan.

We can infer that, since these declarations are absolutes, we cannot doubt their truth, their accuracy. The strategic trends of today all support that all prophetic signs indicate the time is short before we shall experience the biblical predicted end of this age. It shall come to pass as the Lord has prophesied in his word and that is an *absolute truth*. Should the Lord tarry, it will be a blessing to you, and an encouraging influence to seek first the Kingdom of God and all its righteousness, and while there discovering and understanding the precious knowledge of Him and His truths.

I do not want anyone to think that I am trying to prophesy or pass judgment on anyone, or even suggest that anyone not close to God is personally reprehensible and, therefore, spiritually lost. God is the only judge and He has decreed that, "At the fullness of times" (note the plural term), we shall be gathered together one in Christ (The Rapture of His Church). At that time, all saved souls will stand before the judgment seat of Christ, where each of us shall give an account of our compliance to His word, and those chosen by the Lord will be rewarded in accordance with His promises.

This is an Absolute.

It is my heart's fervent desire that everyone finds God's truth, has a full and joyous Christian life, and that eventually will be in the presence of the Lord throughout all eternity. I claim no special expertise that affords me any exclusive insight or answers to all the questions anyone might ask me. However, when I have gone to God with questions, I was guided to His Holy Spirit for leadership. Therefore, it is the hand of God that has guided me to state the truths, the absolutes, of God's words.

I have written these words, often quoting God's *Holy Word*, with a prayer that these words might stimulate a desire within you to seek to know the absolute truth. During the time spent writing this book, I often awakened, having to get up to write what I was hearing some-where deep within me. I personally am neither afraid for what one may think of me after they read this commentary, nor am I ashamed to declare to the entire world what God has truly revealed. I can only have a feeling of humility and thanksgiving for this entire revelation from God. I want to emphasize that Jesus gave us a perfect paradigm, and there is no other.

Understanding God and Jesus

For the past five years I have felt that I had some mission to accomplish. I felt that God wanted me to do something that would contribute positively toward the end harvest.

God surely does not need my help; but, I have fully committed myself to serve Him. Having more time than anything else, I have time to think of how my life definitely has been orchestrated by a very loving God toward some special goal. Meditating on His words and listening, I have a comprehensive accounting of how God protected me from the ever-present fowler, and has revealed to me hidden truths within His written word.

I am writing this to leave following generations an explanation of what I proclaim has been God's freely given blessings, also known as *God's Grace*. Having been widowed three times, I inherited and enjoy an expanded family. A major result of my three marriages is that I now have so many children who call me "Dad" or "Grandpa" and I thought of them as I wrote this book. By describing what God has revealed to me, I hope that I can influence them and others to seek what is the absolute truth. Whoever finds God's truth will also find His wondrous love, the Grace that is abundantly given by God that conquers all and sets us free from this world's bondage. It is because I love every one of my children that I want for them the gift of eternal life.

My Early Quest for Truth

I do know that at an early age, I had both a curiosity about God, and a desire to know for sure what this life was all about. In consultation with the Holy Spirit, I once asked, "Why do some receive healing while others do not, and why does prayer produce miracles for some and not others?"

21

I then began a search of His word and went to prayer to give thanks for His answers. They were plain and easy to understand. Receiving no answer to prayer is the result of both disbelief and disobedience. In Hosea 4:6 God states that because you have rejected knowledge of me and of Jesus, I will reject you that you shall be no priest (or servant) to me. Seeing that you have forgotten my laws, I will also forget your children.

My heavenly Father, during my searching for answers in Your Holy Word, I found that you have revealed it all. It is there in plain sight yet cleverly concealed in mystery, so that to fulfill scripture, one must seek in order to find truth. I realize now, unequivocally, that you are Holy that you have required my totally honest commitment, devotion, obedience, and trust in your inerrant word. The secret ingredient is "faith." Your Holy Spirit counseled me, and led me into a fresh understanding of your truth. It is the absolute truth, for there is none other, which can produce for man a consummation of your abundant grace and mighty and majestic Power.

As it has been revealed to me, written by Isaiah: 53, Jesus did take upon His flesh body all sin and the corruption of evil to die both a physical death and especially a spiritual death for me and all mankind. With all our sins and iniquities borne by Him, Jesus was separated from his Father's Wondrous Love and had to die separated from God's mighty Grace. This is evident when Jesus cried out on the cross, "God, why have thou forsaken me?"

He died the death that has been slated for those who refuse Jesus as Lord and that is why I can say that He truly died for me. Also revealed to me is that the key to prayer is faith that every word uttered by Jesus is the absolute truth. In that Jesus did it all and gave us authority to use his name, and power to those that believe and we will receive gifts. One such gift is that we have available all authority over the weakened power of our enemy. However, though God makes available many spiritual gifts, we must receive them by taking them unto ourselves and, in the authority of His name, put them to work. No gift can help you if you do not accept and apply it, as the Holy Spirit guides you.

Franklin D. Murdock

Learning the Word with God's Guidance

Don't receive my word as gospel, for as it is written, let no man deceive you, but search the scripture for all truth, and the Holy Ghost will fulfill all promises made to and for us, by Jesus. It is well that we realize that God so engineered the Bible as to confuse our adversary and all others that refuse to believe. God classifies the inhabitants of this earth into four categories. They are scoffers, fools, simples, and those that seek wisdom. Three are all losers and the only winner is the one who seeks and finds wisdom (Proverbs 1:31).

Most people I know like a good mystery. Well, herein is more than one and I can tell you that the end of the story is good, so I challenge all who read this to seek the answers for yourselves, and God has even promised to guide you. But to find it you must pick it up, and read your bible. I personally ask you to read the scriptures that I have referenced, but do not think that you, or anyone else, can interpret the meaning of the words in scripture without the help of the true author, the Holy Spirit. Beyond all else, do not take my word as being "gospel," but as it is written, "receive with meekness the engrafted word, and with readiness of mind, and search the scripture daily, whether those things are so" (James 1:21 and Acts17: 11).

So, in answer to my original questions: Do not point fingers and accuse the devil or anyone else, but seek within yourself if you have sought the knowledge of Jesus; and in so doing, establish an intimate relationship with your heavenly daddy, for it is His desire that you are indeed set free from any type of bondage.

After living more than 93 years, I no longer have a "help meet," and being widowed three times, I declare I am at peace in my soul. This I know is a *Blessing and not Presumption.*

---

[1] While I was in prayer, Jesus spoke to me and said that the Bible is the inerrant word of God penned by 40 different men of God as directed by His Holy Spirit, and the Bible is an Absolute. This means it is without error, yet it contains a

23

mystery of God's purpose pertaining to life. Even though man has attempted to simplify and make its meanings easier to understand, through the many versions of the scriptures, or by man's attempt to interpret the meaning of the original translated word using only his own efficiency without the guidance of the Holy Spirit, he has only succeeded in superimposing a noise factor to the true word. It is with great sorrow that an element of vanity was born into man's generated religion due to the lack of purity of knowledge of God and of God's master plan and the true purpose of the ministry of Jesus.]

CHAPTER 3

God: His Character and Nature

First, I would like to attempt to define God and His character and nature. I cannot do this without relying on and making reference to scientific and or historical facts; but only if they are illuminated by the wisdom of God. It is of interest to note that the famous Albert Einstein, as a child, was denied schooling because he could not learn, or so his teachers claimed. He did not even have a formal high school education, and only after repeated efforts did he pass an entrance examination to a university. Yet, without question, relevant to this world's limited intellect, he had a brilliant mind.

Now let us consider the creation of our "mind-boggling" universe. First we note that God spoke things into existence because of the power of the spoken word in the spiritual universe. He spoke the worlds into existence from "nothing," or did He? What the scripture reveals is the awesome majestic power that God has. He is omnipotent and omniscient, having full command over mass, energy, light, and time. Writing of, and referring to sciences, will include physics, chemistry, astronomy, genetic engineering (DNA), mathematics, and probably the most important and less understood: quantum physics and quantum mechanics. The name "quantum theory" comes from the fact that the theory describes the matter and energy in the universe in terms of single, indivisible units called quanta.

I understand very little about quantas but so do many of our top scientists. They know what quantas are and that they work, but they cannot explain every function. Oddly enough, without quantum physics and mechanics, we would not have what is commonly accepted and known as today as integrated circuits that make possible our high-speed computers, and space exploration sciences. What we take for granted are all the amenities offered by today's technologies, and very few people ever realize the complexity of the technology employed in the medical field, and medicines in agriculture and our food supply. Technology is so vital in our everyday society, yet most if not all of us are ignorant of how much of this works. We use cell phones, the internet, facebook, and twitter, all navigated through the use of satellites and take these convenient communications for granted, because of our lack of understanding.

Mysteries of Science and God

Here are some fundamental examples of quantum physics and mechanics, and some pertinent questions:

1. Put a kettle of water on the stove and put heat under it. It will soon boil dry. Has the   water been destroyed, or has it only taken on another form; and, if so, where did it go?

2. Take a box, set in a clear area, and set it on fire. Let it burn until there is nothing left but dry ash. As it burned there were elements of smoke, moisture, and gases that disappeared into the atmosphere, and what is left is only ash. Were the elements that made up the atomic or the molecular structure destroyed? No, but man does not have the capability that God has to gather all the elements that constituted the gases and smoke back, and to combine them in proper quantity with the ashes to re-create that box. But God has that capability. Think of this as you think of the promised resurrection.

1. Let's take a 12-inch ruler and divide it into two equal six-inch parts. Discard one of them. Then progressively divide the smaller half by two. One might think that you could divide this to some infinitesimal value. However, science has established a

26

finite number, beyond which there is no descriptive value in length, mass, energy, or time in seconds that can be made smaller. It is known in scientific communities as a quantum, an indivisible unit. For length that value is 10 to the minus 33rd power in centimeters, and is known as the *Planck length.* This will constitute sub-atomic particles. For time, there is a unit of value equal to 10 to the minus 43rd power in seconds (a point 1 with 43 zeroes after the point and before the 1). Today's scientific communities have encountered strange environments of subatomic behavior. It is the study of the boundaries and characteristics of these subatomic mechanisms that is known as *quantum physics or mechanics.* What spurred those behaviors?

King Solomon wrote in Ecclesiastes 1:9, "That which has been is what will be; and that which is done is what shall be done: and there is no new thing under the sun." Now consider for review what I just discussed scientifically above. We know these things, though we cannot explain or understand them. Thus, even the scientifically observable phenomena in our world are mysterious and not fully explainable.

Regarding God, it has been stated, written, and preached that in the word of God, the Bible reveals the nature of God. He is both unity, and trinity. He is a spirit, a personal infinite being. He is one, one in substance or nature, and incapable of being divided into separate parts. He is three eternally, existing in three co-equal persons: God the Father, God the Son, and God the Holy Spirit. Using words to describe God's attributes is not possible, for He exists in eternity, and exists or lives in multiple dimensions beyond our intellect or understanding. God is omniscience, all knowing, He cannot learn anything new for He already knows all (a real know-it-all!) He is omnipresence, all present, being everywhere at the same time. He is omnipotence, all power existing in and with him. But there is more: God exists outside our limited dimensions, for we are incapable of understanding all that He is. Just as we are incapable of fully comprehending everything about

27

quantum mechanics and physics, we cannot fully comprehend what God is.

We live in a three-dimensional world and understand something of a fourth dimension. God lives in what scientists of theology today have estimated as being ten dimensions or more. If we could comprehend a geographical place where time does not exist, we would find that there abides God, and He was there even before time existed. That place is eternity and is permanent. (Just think, we will share that eternity with Him after the fullness of time.) Time did not begin until God spoke it into existence when He commanded, "Light be", and then divided the light from darkness, and the evening and the morning were the first day. Notice that the evening came before the first morning. At least one researcher studying Genesis in the 12th century determined and so declared that before that instant, there was no time. The impact has the connotation that an extensive period yet undefined could have elapsed between "the beginning" and ending of the "first day." This could also have the connotation that this earth home was created for man. Before sin corrupted, it was in reality part of eternity, and will be again, according to chapter 22 in Revelation.

God as the author engineered the composition of His message. We know it as His Bible, and He originated it outside of our time domain. It is appropriate to know that many illustrious scientists have established that time is a physical property, and is affected and varies with mass, acceleration, and gravity. This has been proven by measurements of the interaction characteristics of sub-atomic particles, the speed of light, and measurements made with two identical atomic clocks. The clocks were set to the exact same time, then subjected to flights around our world, one going from west to east, while the other going east to west. They found that the time indicated by the two clocks was affected by acceleration, altitude, and the direction of flight around the earth.

We now learn from our scientific community that our universe is quantumized. This means it is digital, and is reduced to the smallest indivisible value, thus being an observable quality or portion. Yet, to date, we are unable to accurately define or predict this indivisible unit.

So we must ask, "Is God affected by gravity, acceleration, or mass?" Of course, He is not. For eternity is outside our physical dimension of time and mass. Isaiah 57:15 states: "For thus say the high and lofty one that inhabits eternity, whose name is Holy, I dwell in the high and holy place....." The Majesty of God is so startling and awesome that we mortals cannot comprehend or have more than a meager glimpse of His Deity.

This is what I will attempt to define: If all matter exists in some form no matter how infinitesimal, God had to create it in the beginning. God having all power, He commanded these particles to obey, and they formed the matter that is our created universe. It would not make any difference to me if He used a "Big Bang" to accomplish His word or not. I personally do not believe that He did. Hebrews 11:3 states: "By faith we understand that the worlds were framed by the word of God, so that the things which are seen were not made of things which are visible."

The overwhelming power that is God's is far beyond our capacity of understanding, but it is so reassuring when you know Him and know that He is right here with you and me at all times. I ask you, "Do you have any doubt or is there any wonder that He is God?" Let us not make God and Jesus a religion and try bringing them from their High and Holy place to this corrupted environment known as this world. It is essential at this stage of spiritual maturity that we continue searching the scripture for the absolute truth concerning the personage of God.

Forty men of God, covering a period over five thousand years, did write with inspiration from God, sixty-six books that are the origin of the Bible. Although they were written in three different languages, there is only one author. It is an intimate love letter from our heavenly daddy composed so majestically that it is applicable to every soul inhabiting this earth today, for it is a living word, although most will either deny it, or will never read it. It is idiomatically composed, having numerous, cleverly concealed messages within each statement or story.

The Nature of God

I think we all have asked this question, and I found the only way to receive an answer while seeking truth is by studying Him. That means dedicating priority time to study His Word.

For most of my life I, too, pondered the question of "who is God" and "how can I get to know Him?" There was the time when I was much younger, about 12 years old, and I would dress for the occasion to meet Him and travel to more affluent neighborhoods to attend some church services, hoping to find the individual my mother had told me about. But I never found Him in any of the churches I visited. I was looking for Him to materialize when all the time He was as close as my breath; but I knew Him not. I knew of him and even prayed the prayer of faith my mother had taught me. I experienced His visitations but, until I seriously began studying Him (his word), my mind was blinded by the God of this world. I witnessed firsthand the havoc and death that engulfed this world during World War II. I personally felt His presence many times; but I would not have been able to define His nature or character, let alone His master plan for redemption and glorification.

Yet during his visitation in that hospital room in 1981, He said: "I want you to find out all you can about me, my character and nature." We are taught that He is love and is full of compassion and grace. He also tells us that He is a jealous God, and demands obedience. This is true but is not the whole truth. He is identified in Psalms 91 as "the most high" almighty God, and in John 3:16 is proclaimed a truth. In the King James version, God is described thus: "He so loves the world that He gave His only begotten son, and that whosoever believes in him should have everlasting life." This declaration has more than one meaning and I will attempt to explain it, as God has revealed to me the wondrous message concealed in these words. First of all, He could have left out the word "so," but that word contains volumes of meaning.

30

The Holy Spirit of God revealed that it should be acknowledged as very personal as we assess the value of life. Read it like this: "God loves me, or God loves you, or Mary, or Robert so much that it outweighed the love He had for His only begotten son. He allowed His only begotten son to be so horribly and brutally scourged (beaten) then crucified unto death just so He could have a personal and loving relationship with us and have it for eternity."

This is only a part of the mysteries related to the word "so," for His beloved son was on another mission. That was to destroy all the works of Satan and to take from him the keys he had made to death and hell after he stole God's blessing from Adam. By doing this His son Jesus took upon himself all sin and corruption past, present, and future. In so doing He redeemed all who accept Him from being condemned by sin, and God no longer imputes punishment for innocent sin; however, the consequences may result in actions by Satan, not by God. By so doing He has provided the way for the world God so loved to find the key to His Kingdom and establish and nurture that intimate relationship that God "so" desires to be manifest with His created man, reuniting man with Him as it was in the beginning.

In John 3:16 also note the word "should." It does not say "will have" as a guarantee. Yes, He desires for every man to prosper as his soul prospers and to have life more abundantly. He has provided for each of us a way to attain that goal. It is through the blood that was shed by Jesus, for there is no other way.

His first commandment is that we must love him with our entire heart, soul, and mind. I ask you, is that too much for us to commit ourselves to Him after what He has done for us? We can do it now and prosper as our soul prospers, or take the chance of making it through the tribulation, and have to attain this attribute during the millennial age.

Studying His character has revealed that He has feelings just as you and me; but He has perfect patience up to a point that his word defines it as "the appointed" time, or the fullness of days. Even though you rightly know Him as love, he also hates.

31

Proverbs 6:16-19 depict six things He hates and the seventh thing that is an abomination to him. They are:

- Haughty eyes
- A lying tongue
- Hands that kill the innocent
- A heart that plots evil
- Feet that race to do wrong
- A false witness that pours out lies
- A person who sows or causes discord among his family, or brothers

So, even though God is love, his love cannot tolerate the evils that are listed above. God wants us to be righteous and upstanding. This requires not only abstaining from the evils He abhors, but it also requires knowing what God wants of us.

To know Him, we must diligently immerse ourselves in the study of his word. That sounds easy, and you may think because you go to a church one or two times a week, sing in the church choir, or even play the organ or piano through the praise program, that you satisfy God, and you are religious, and will be accepted unto God to receive all blessings. I'm sorry to have to tell you that you may not really know Him. I am sure that you will agree with me that He has declared that in the beginning was the word, and the word was with God, and the word was God. If the word was God, it still is, for God has not changed. Therefore, I ask you: How can you know Him if you never pick up your Bible to study his instructions and precepts? For to know him is to love him, and to love him enflames a desire to want to gain and understand all the forgotten or lost knowledge of Him and of his son Jesus.

Preparing for the Future

Now to apply all this to this book, *The Best Is Yet to Come.* I know that God desires all men to come to the fullness of the knowledge of Him and Jesus, and repentance so as to be saved and inherit all that He has for us. We are informed that God's wrath will be poured out during the upcoming tribulation. Wrath from an all-forgiving and loving God? Yes, that is exactly what we have been told. All you need to read is Genesis 6 where it depicts God as being deeply grieved by man allowing sin to dominate his life, and there being no room for God. Yes, He has emotions just as you and I have. I have shown you where in scripture he will send the inhabitants of earth a strong delusion to believe a lie. Believing that lie will bring into manifestation a world rent with all the anger and evil conjured by Satan, and God will withdraw himself, and you might say as Jesus said on the cross, "Why have you forsaken me?"

He has given all men the fullness of days to conform to His spiritual world; but, just as the early Israelites that had only the law to guide them, they failed to obey His laws or instructions, yet they are still the apple of His eye and will be forever more. Therefore, to prepare for the implementation and establishment of His Kingdom on Earth, all discord and evil must be purged; but, to really know Him is as He has declared, in John 6:14: "Those who drink of the water I give will never be thirsty again. It becomes a fresh, bumbling spring within them, giving them eternal life" (New Living Translation). The next step is to develop a strong and intimate relationship with our loving, true Father, then to have it mature into a loving, perpetual fellowship that you can exhibit trust without wavering, building each day faith everlasting.

There is one more thing that I must reveal. Many religious denominations preach doctrine, "that healing or miracles only refers to the apostolic age, and is not applicable today." That is a lie of Satan, for the apostolic age has never stopped. In the beginning of this book, I list persons of God that I recognize as contributing to my ever-growing, personal spiritual maturity. These are all sent by God to reveal His nature and fulfill His purpose, so these people are in reality apostles. God has proclaimed in His word, that He chooses those He wishes to be His servants, calling them from the womb of their mother, thereafter forming and shaping them to accomplish their calling. To

The Best is Yet to Come

God be all the glory, and to each producing servant I give my humble thanks.

CHAPTER 4

Sin and Satan

After approximately 34 years of experiencing that life-changing visitation in the hospital, and receiving some knowledge of truth, I questioned the Holy Spirit about the origin of sin and the birth of Satan. I reminded Him that God wanted me to know all about my adversary. I was more than just a little confused, for as it is stated in John 1:3, "All things were made by him; and without him was not anything made that was made."

I have continually been in an attitude of prayer petitioning God and my Lord Jesus to reveal through his word truth concerning my pondering. Recently, while I was lying on my bed meditating and thinking of the things happening, I felt a stirring in my spirit, recognizing that feeling of complete serenity. I knew it was the Holy Spirit of God speaking to me, since I was pondering on the subject of Satan and sin, and longing for direction to comprehend and understand the truth about my adversary, its origin, and where and how did it originate? Why did God, who had a perfect environment in His heaven, create, if He did, the spirit of evil, Satan the devil? Then create this earth and all the galaxies in the second heaven, and fine-tune their physical properties so that their interfacing influence on each other would hold them all in harmony. Then God cast that evil spirit into that earth where its corrupt influence could reign throughout this whole creation. After this, God came to earth himself in the likeness of a son to overcome this evil, while all the time preparing for him, and all man who have chosen curses and death over blessings and life (Deuteronomy 30:19), along with setting a place for the final demise of the fallen angels. At the beginning of the creation of man we know the earth was without form and was void of life. Then God had His Holy Spirit, the Holy Ghost, move over the face of the earth and separate the waters from land. God then made his garden, located west of Eden.

It was perfect in all ways and is a picture of what God intends for his created human family, and it will be again after his kingdom has physically been established on earth, that will be accomplished during the millennium rein of Jesus. Remember the Lord's Prayer: "Thy Kingdom come, Thy will be done." It has been declared by Jesus, and will come to pass, and that is an absolute statement.

I now will share what the spirit revealed to me. I questioned, what all does the scripture reveal about this, that is still not understood, and not being taught? I heard the voice within me say, "Go back to the beginning," so I began thinking of the creation of man, Adam and Eve, and their placement in the Garden of Eden. The voice said, "No! Go back further," so I thought of His creation of the heavens and earth. That is exactly where he wanted me to begin, before the foundation of this world and the creation of man.

The Emergence of Sin and Evil

The Holy Spirit wanted me to have a more comprehensive understanding of the real beginning, His kingdom existing in the third heaven located beyond our outer space, or outside the realm of all galaxies. It has existed before the creation of the first and second heavens, including the earth. It radiates His perfect love. This love will manifest His glory in man culminating in the ultimate utopia through the absolute unity and integrity of His earthly kingdom. It is destined on this earth for eternity in a purged and purified new world. All this manifests after the annihilation of Satan and all evil on this earth.

I asked the spirit that was talking to me: "Was the evil spirit identified as Satan the devil, made by God, and if so why?" I could not comprehend that God could or would purposely create anything so

vile. If the evil spirit we know as Satan was not created, is he an alien
spirit that was able to infiltrate the dominion of heaven and there
corrupt even the cherished anointed cherub of God that was his
personal covering angel? His answer to me was, "No, he is not a
purposeful creation, nor is he an alien spirit. He was my anointed
angel; but, since Satan has become manifest through the iniquity of
this angel into a spirit of evil, he has to be dealt with in judgment,
which is meticulously delineated within the written word."

The answer to how Satan became manifest is found in Ezekiel
28, which alludes to Satan being the product by the power of the sinful
actions and power of the spoken words of the treasonous renegade
angel identified only as the anointed cherub. Many so-called
fundamental religions and evangelists teach that this angel's name is
Lucifer. However, my search of all scripture revealed that Lucifer
refers to a place, such as Tyre, or Babylon, or perhaps an identifiable
place or office of responsibility in God's Heavenly Kingdom wherein
the anointed cherub who was the sum of all wisdom, and all
subordinate angels that were cast out of Heaven, abided and served
God as the giver of light. But Lucifer was not the name of an angel.
This is the result of man attempting to interpret God's word without
the help of His Holy Spirit, and was wrongly adopted by religious men
in the 3rd century AD. Isaiah 14:12 seems to identify this anointed
cherub as Lucifer, Son of the Morning Star, A Giver of Light. The
word *anointed* in this case indicates that he held a very high office
with a lot of authority. The phrases "Morning Star" and "Giver of
Light" in the Hebrew language are translated to "Lucifer," but
nowhere in scriptures does the Word identify this anointed cherub by
name. Therefore, the name Lucifer is a translation of phrases, not a
translated word.

It is written in 2 Peter 1:20 that no prophecy of scripture is for
private interpretation. This fallen angel's belligerent arrogance and his
self-imposed unrighteousness were the source from which Satan and
sin were born. God depicted him in Ezekiel 28: 12-14 as the king of
Tyre. This may allude to a mortal man possessed by the spirit of Satan,
but that is presumption only. It is written, "As a man (or angel) thinks

in his heart, so is he." Therefore Satan is a separate and unique creation manifested by the transformation of God's once-anointed cherub. He once represented the epitome of wisdom and beauty in God's Kingdom in heaven and was anointed to serve the throne of God; but, by his arrogance, pride, and self-exaltation was transformed by the power of his spoken word and his self-applied iniquity into absolute evil.

The spirit then told me that man and angels were created with the same free spirit. He instructed me to meditate on this in order that I could comprehend and understand the basis of the origin of evil. It is important to realize that man and angels are created with a free spirit, with free choice; but, angels are created having eternal life, while man is created a little lower as a mortal. For God to have limited this freedom can be likened to the habit of man breaking the spirit of a wild animal to be a useful serving beast, or what we call domesticated, so the creature is no longer free. The Holy Spirit informed me that this freedom has a built-in frailty. This requires implicit dedication and self-control to overcome its vulnerability to temptations with all its consequences, unless totally mastered from within, such as was done by Jesus, our perfect example.

No, God did not make a mistake when He created and anointed his cherished cherub. All mankind, both male and female, are vulnerable to the same fallacy. In God's earthly kingdom there is to be no division like that which came to pass in God's Holy habitat when His covering angel became alienated from the virtue of love that bonds heaven into the secret place of the most high God, with a oneness of spirit having love for one another.

The Mystery of Life

Herein is the mystery of life: As Jesus stated, the Kingdom of God is within us and we must cultivate this love to maturity. Likewise, because of sin, so is the kingdom of this world within each of us. By our individual choices it becomes possible for us to birth in our lives a personal Satan that will dominate our life through sin, which will hinder or block our ability to receive all blessings from our Heavenly Father, resulting in our destruction. This can never happen if you confess Jesus as Lord of your life, and relinquish all selfness to Him and put your trust in God; but, as long as Satan is active in this world, he will not tire attempting to lure you into sin.

Adam and his wife Eve seemed to have had it made, because the perfect peace and love of God was part of their inheritance. Adam was given a crown of Glory and placed in God's garden to maintain and dress it. In the garden were two trees, the tree of knowledge of good and evil, and the tree of life. Adam was instructed by God, not to partake of the fruit from the tree of knowledge but was not prohibited from eating the fruit from the tree of life.

What happened? Adam and Eve were deceived by the evil spirit birthed in the renegade angel, and they were deceived and partook of that forbidden fruit. Before the iniquity was found in him, this angel while still abiding in heaven, had the authority of strolling among the precious stones in the Garden of Eden. He is now my adversary and therefore man's adversary also. The origin of sin and the birth of Satan originated in the kingdom of heaven by the actions and spoken word from that same renegade angel.

The Holy Spirit then reminded me again, it is most important to realize that, as this happened to an angel, it can also happen to man. We see this every day as people are subject to all the maladies suffered, none of which are the result of direct action of God. We have all believed the deceitful lies of Satan that these maladies are intended to strengthen our faith in God. You only have to study the life of Jesus during His earthly ministry to realize that His doing the will of the Father denied no one from healing. Yes, it is possible that by our belief and spoken word we can bind ourselves in bondage to the master of all deceit, Satan. Remember God's word of instruction in Genesis 4:7, that Satan wants to destroy you to offend me; but, you must master him. (This sounds like a commandment, for mankind has no other choice in order to be acceptable unto God.)

The Best is Yet to Come

At this point in my story I think it is important to express the truth concerning the power we have in our tongue. Matthew 12:34-37 declares whatever thoughts are in our heart, we will speak, and for every word spoken, even idle words, we must give an account on judgment day. For by the words we speak, we will either be justified or condemned. Likewise, in Proverbs 18:21 we are informed that we have the power of death or life in our tongue. The power in spoken words is well defined within God's word.

Relevant to this is Romans 12:2, which tells us that being evil shows conformity to this material world; and to be transformed into the spiritual realm of God's world, we must renew our mind, for this is how we can overcome the spirit of evil. This evil must be purged from all my creation.

After the Angel Michael fought a war with Satan and his subordinate angels, they all were cast out of heaven into the earth until final judgment can be rendered. In Revelation 12:12 the word informs us that at the time of Satan's expulsion from the Kingdom of Heaven, there were inhabitants of the earth, and God's words warn all peoples of the earth with these words, "Woe to the inhibiters of the earth and sea! For the devil will come down unto you, having great wrath, because he knows that he has but a short time." God said "woe" unto man meaning an exclamation of grief, and putting more emphasis on mankind's imperative to master evil.

At the same time in Revelation 12:10, there was a rejoicing in Heaven for "now is come salvation, and strength, and the Kingdom of our God, and the power of His Christ." This predicts that the best is yet to come.[1]

Other Revelations by the Holy Spirit Regarding Sin

I continued to receive divine knowledge as the Holy Spirit continued. He said: "Adam's failure to keep my commandment was an act of disobedience and is considered sinful; but is not the full definition of sin. By this disobedience, sin was introduced not only

40

into Adam's and Eve's personal life and all their future descendants; but because Adam had been given complete dominion over this creation, the entire world become subject and enslaved to its evil forces."

So just what is sin? It is the inability to accept unequivocally, trust in our Father to provide all our needs abundantly (Matthew 18:3). It is the sum total of all the corruption, pestilence, and afflictions with all their grief and pain, man's greed and selfishness, that contaminates all life in, beneath, on, and above the earth until it is finally judged and permanently purged from earth, and from accepted and reborn man, and all heavenly places.

I was reminded that it had not taken God very long after Adam's disobedience to make known just what man's personal responsibility was. Being first reminded that God had expelled from His heavenly kingdom the evil devil Satan, and all his demonic angels, I was reminded in order for man to be accepted (sanctified), man must rule, or master, sin and not let Satan be his master. That advice is applicable to you and me this very day. In answer to my question, how, God then revealed to me that in order that we might master sin, it is imperative we apprehend and comprehend ourselves having the spirit and power of His Holy Spirit. He put this into us as we experienced the new birth, then, most importantly, the renewing of our mind. This infusion with the Holy Spirit enables us to effectively use every spiritual tool that He has provided.

Knowing that we on our own do not have the efficiency to overcome the adversary, He declared that He would never forsake us nor leave us alone and unprotected with this battle, and by personal experience, I know He is faithful to keep His promises. His word is our mighty weapon, and I cannot over-emphasize the words "mighty weapon" that are for the overthrowing and the destruction of spiritual strongholds that impede us (2 Corinthians 10:3-6).

Although our adversary is invisible, we have the authority, using the words of God, as Jesus did when tempted by Satan for forty days and nights, to defeat our enemy. The Holy Spirit then brought to my attention that He has informed us in His word that we must not be lackadaisical and think that because we have accepted Jesus as our Lord and have received the filling of the Holy Spirit that we have a free pass or have it made and have nothing more to do to master sin. In Deuteronomy 7:11-12, God states that we shall keep and do His instructions, live in accordance with His law, and honor all that He has commanded of us in order to receive the light of His countenance upon us, and gain favor with Him and master sin. This requires we commit our entire heart, soul, and mind to gaining the true knowledge of God and Jesus by submerging self into His word.[2]

As I pondered on all that God was revealing to me, He reminded me that I am tri-part—flesh, soul, and spirit—and because of sin being dominant in this world since Adam succumbed to it, and Satan was cast out of heaven, we all are born having a sinful nature in our flesh body which will continually lust against the spirit He planted in us. This is why we have inherent within us a relationship with Satan. At the same time we are not to have a fellowship with him. For this reason God recognizes that at times we have difficulty discerning His will in our lives, but the spirit He put in us is greater than the spirit of all darkness. Speaking to my spirit, God then informed me that I need to be diligent and study so that I can affirmatively and rightly separate truth from untruth, which is widely prevalent through all the media and many religious churches today. God tells us to study the word to rightly separate truth from untruth (2 Timothy 2:15) and at all times be aware of the ever-present Satan, for he is real. He wants every created man, but we must learn to rule and master him.

None of this negates the covenant of Grace. We are saved by the atoning blood of Jesus; but in order that we be raised up and sanctified, it is important this, too, shall be accomplished. Satan and this iniquity are alien to God's kingdoms and will be judged. "You are my beloved and are destined to inherit all that is mine," says the Lord.

In two places in scripture God's word declares: "In the last days I will pour out My Spirit on all mankind, and your sons and daughters shall prophesy and your young men will see visions, and your old men shall dream (divinely suggested) dreams." These prophecies are recorded in the following scripture: Joel 2:28 written about 830 years BC, and in Acts 2:17, written by Luke in the 1st century AD. I make reference to these scriptures to emphasize the seriousness of today's worldly environment.

Although I spent many hours listening to the Holy Spirit, I say even though I am elderly, I was not dreaming. This may be somewhat controversial to some of you. If so I suggest you take it up with the true authority, the author of all scripture, the Holy Spirit. I strongly recommend you program your mind with the Word of God. The Word is spirit and it is life with healing to our flesh, and our mighty weapon for defeating our adversary. When your mind is totally saturated with the Word of God, your will becomes strong to exercise authority to overcome every ungodly thought and evil habit, casting down all imaginary visions that do not promote God's glory and plan.

Besides, it will better prepare you for the changes to come.

---

[1] This gives credence to a scientific document I had the privilege of hearing that alleged God created the heavens and earth for a reason. First, to provide an environment where Satan and all fallen angels could be incarcerated until final judgment could be rendered, as stated in Rev. 12:12 above. These principalities and powers of evil are the spiritual enemies of God and man with which we are in our minds continually at war, and shall by the renewing of our minds be able by the power of the Holy Spirit to master Satan's evil; but, we must continually recognize they are angelic and therefore very powerful and enduring. Secondly, to provide a permanent home, or castle not made with hands, for his beloved children in his kingdom on earth after they are sanctified, as Rev. 12:10 alluded.

[2] As a personal footnote, although this is in the Torah of the Old Testament, we who have been born again and received our new spirit, and thereby made a new creature in Christ Jesus, were then grafted into His family and therefore all scriptures apply equally to all of us, whether Jew or Gentile. It is a truth that in the Old Testament, the New Testament is concealed; and in the New Testament, the Old Testament is revealed. The whole Bible is one integrated message, and we cannot comprehend and understand our Father's instructions and His precepts without thoroughly studying both.

The Best is Yet to Come

CHAPTER 5

Deceived Religious Dogma

On September 11, 2001, America was attacked by foreign organized militia destroying the World Trade Center in New York and attacking the Pentagon in Washington, D.C. This act, planned and perpetrated by terrorists, killed more than three-thousand civilians. As a result, our President, with the fervent backing of the American people, declared a war against the responsible organized terrorists, and perhaps not understood, was backed by Congress and declared war against general worldwide terror. What are we up against, and what is the real issue? We need some understanding of the origin, nature, and agenda of any order that harbors such evil against any inhabitants of this earth. Those responsible for the attack on September 11 were all of the Muslim religion, the nation of Islam. By their action attacking civilian and commercial targets, the terrorists openly declared the start of their Jihad, a religious war to create such total catastrophic environments worldwide that their God Allah would manifest their lost or hidden savior that would put an end to the torment and establish an everlasting kingdom of Islam. At the same time, Islam would annihilate all peoples and religions not accepting

The Best is Yet to Come

Islam as their faith, and especially western culture in the world.
Unfortunately, there are in the world today both religious and political
leaders who have declared that they have a divine mission from their
God Allah to start the great and last war.

When the former president of Iran, Mahmoud Ahmadinejad, addressed the United Nations General Assembly in October of 2005, he ended his speech with a prayer imploring Allah to hasten the return of the 12th Imam. He referred to this Imam, also known as the Mahdi, in almost all his major speeches. In the Islamic faith, the Mahdi is the ultimate savior of mankind. His appearance will usher in an era of Islamic justice and bring about the conversion of the heathen amidst flame and fire.

The Mahdi will establish Islam as the global religion and will reign for seven years before bringing about the end of the world. In a speech, the president of Iran is quoted as saying: "Our revolution's main mission is to pave the way for the reappearance of the 12th Imam, the Mahdi. Therefore, Iran should become a powerful, developed, and model Islamic society. Today, we should define our economic, cultural and political policies based on the policy of Imam Mahdi's return. We should avoid copying the West's policies and systems."

The beliefs of Sunni and Shiite Muslims differ on the identity of the Mahdi. Sunnis either believe that he is yet to be born, or that he was born recently and has yet to emerge. Shiites hold that the Mahdi is Muhammad Hasan, a descendant of the Prophet Muhammad born in the 9th century and the 12th and final Shiite Imam. As a devout Shiite, the Iranian president believes that the 12th Imam was hidden away by Allah at a young age and will someday emerge to bring justice and peace by establishing Islam throughout the world. Ahmadinejad ardently believed in the imminent return of the 12th Imam, which he anticipated would happen by the year 2013. He believed he had a personal role in ushering in the return of the Mahdi and did all he could to prepare Iran for Judgment Day.

46

Fortunately for our world, Ahmadinejad is no longer the president of Iran, and the recent Iranian presidential elections resulted in the victory of a perceived moderate cleric, Hassan Rouhani, who, so far, appears to be far more peaceful toward our country and other nations of the world. Time will judge whether or not Iran moves away from its belligerent path toward violent Islamic domination of the planet and toward peaceful co-existence with all nations, all races, and all religions. Hopefully this will be the case.

The Militant Islamic Threat to the World

Understanding Ahmadinejad's perspective is vital to our comprehending the threat that faces our nation and the rest of the world, particularly non-Muslim nations. The continuing Afghanistan War and the continued turbulence and violence in Iraq after our departure from the war there still reverberate throughout the world, particularly in the Middle East. Ramifications from that horrible violence affected and continue to harm our nation's people and well-being.

These wars and other conflicts first stemming from the September 11 attack on our nation are, ultimately, wars of ideology. This war between Islam and other religions really began about 4,500 years ago with anger between the children of Abraham, Ishmael, the twin sons of his son of the promise Isaac, his grandsons Esau and Jacob. Ishmael and the twin brother Esau are the fathers of all Arabic nationals who have an undying hate for any descendants of Jacob. Jacob, renamed Israel by an angel of God, is the father of all Jews and the spiritual father of all Christians. The writing in the Bible is the foundation of Christianity, while the Arab Muslims adopted a religion of their own derived from the writings of Moses, the Psalms, and an alleged prophet named Muhammad who wrote their "holy" book titled the Qur'an (pronounced "Koran"). It was written in the 7th century after the Holy Bible had been written.

The Qur'an is declared by the Muslim nations to have superseded the Bible and therefore is the only true word. It is the foundation for the Muslim faith. It is important that we are not blindsided by either politically correct propaganda or an overzealous news media. I believe it is important that we understand all we can learn about our adversary, not necessarily the Muslim people, who may merely be his victims. Yet be not deceived, unless all Muslims forsake the instructions taught by their "Holy Book" the Qur'an and accept Jesus as the living son of the true and only God. Radical Muslims—sometimes called "Islamists" in today's political environment—are committed to fight for, and kill if they think it necessary, for the preservation and promotion of Islam. It is important to remember that the majority of Muslims in the world are peaceful, but the extremist Muslims are almost always the ones who get international attention for their violence and terrorism. These are the Muslims behind Al Qaeda, the terror group that attacked our nation and that supports death and violence in the name of Islam all over the world. There are many other terrorist organizations now, but these are run by extremist, often fundamentalist, Muslims who do not represent all the Islamic people of earth.

The first questions often asked about this conflict with Islam that has caused the deaths of hundreds of thousands of people worldwide are Why does God allow this to happen? and Why do they, the fanatical religious Islamic followers, hate us and America? First of all, do not overlook the fact that when Adam surrendered to Satan, he that anointed angels then became the god of this world, whose goal was to create as much hate among the inhabitants as possible. What better way than to use religious dogma to create mind-controlled hate? I have heard reports allegedly made by Arabic secular news that about 15,000 Muslims a day are converting to Christianity.

To answer why we are hated, Jesus is quoted in John 15:19, saying, "If you were of this world, the world would love his own; but, I have chosen you out of the world; therefore, the world hates you." Secondly, the followers of Muhammad are taught that Jesus is not the Son of God because of this belief in their religion being of this world.

48

It grieves God that most who claim to know Him, have not bothered to even try understanding the Bible, let alone anything about the Qur'an, which is the only book used by all Muslims. Their Koran is a book of doctrine, and is their religious foundation. Islam dates back to the pagan worship of the Moon God. Their beloved prophet Muhammad founded the religion, as we know it today.

The Muslims believe Muhammad was the "final" prophet, who was taken by the Angel Gabriel, sent by their God they call Allah to escort him through six different levels of heaven, to their most High God in the seventh heaven. In our Bible in 2 Corinthians 12:2, the kingdom of God is in the third heaven.

The Qur'an states Muhammad met Allah in the seventh heaven, where Muhammad communed with Allah and learned of his true purpose. Among other things, the Qur'an teaches that it is a lie that God ever took to Himself a son (Jesus). That Jesus, the son of Mary, was not the Son of God but was a prophet born by natural process. It also teaches that all Jews and Christians are the enemy of Allah. Muhammad may have surely had a spiritual visitation, but wherever it was, it was not from Jehovah God. For a clearer understanding, it is noteworthy that the Qur'an is comprised of five articles of faith, which are the main doctrines of Islam. All Muslims are expected to believe and adopt the following:

1. GOD: There is one true God and his name is Allah.
2. ANGELS: Angels exist and interact with human lives. They are comprised of light, and each has different purposes or messages to bring to earth. Each man and woman has two angels who record their actions; one records good deeds, the other bad deeds.
3. SCRIPTURE: There are four inspired books—the Torah of Moses, the Psalms of David, the Gospel of Jesus Christ (Injil), and the Qur'an (Koran). Stated in the latter is the following: "All but the Qur'an has been corrupted by Jews and Christians."

49

4. PROPHETS: God has spoken through numerous prophets throughout time. The six greatest are Adam, Noah, Abraham, Moses, Jesus, and Muhammad. Muhammad is the last and the greatest of Allah's messengers.

5. LAST DAYS: On the last day there will be a time of resurrection and judgment.

A sixth religious duty associated with the five pillars is *Jihad*, or *Holy War*. This duty requires that if the situation warrants, all men of Islam are required to fight (go to war) in order to defend or to spread Islam. Those who follow Allah and Muhammad will go to Islamic heaven, or paradise. Those who do not will go to hell. If they are killed performing their sacred duty, they are guaranteed eternal life in paradise. It also teaches that in order to go to Islamic heaven, one must kill a Jew, a Christian, or an unbeliever called an infidel. Perhaps this will reveal a better understanding of what Christianity and our fighting forces are facing. Not all Muslims follow every letter of the Qur'an any more than those that declare they are Christians follow every word in the Bible, although they should.

The above defines the basic beliefs of all Muslims delineated in their "Holy Koran," which is more a battle manual than a holy book. Therefore, the fundamentals of the Islamic culture are vastly different from what the Christian Bible teaches.

Muhammad wrote new guidelines for Islam, allegedly from God. The Koran does not even mention the word "love" but teaches and advocates violence. Admittedly, the Bible also has many sections involving wars and killings of innocent people, references to human sacrifice, and other unsettling elements invoking violence. But Christianity is based on love, not violence and forced religious conversion upon pain of death. Many believe that Islam is one of the few, if not the only, world religion, that clearly advocates violence and death in its name. This portends ill for the prospects for peace and harmony throughout our planet, and for the fate of our world at large.

Other Religions and Their Deviations

Studying the origins and doctrines of other religions, one can find many deviations from the basic teaching of Jesus, and I do not intend to imply that any are incomprehensible or, for Jesus shed His blood for all of us.

The Catholic Church

The Catholic religion, a Christian faith, teaches followers certain doctrines that are not supported by the word of God as written in the Bible. In fact, the Catholic religion is based less on the Bible than it is on their missals (books of prayers); distinct rituals in their religious service, called a "mass"; and various proclamations or guidelines delivered by the Vatican in Rome, Italy, the world headquarters of Catholicism. The Catholic Bible is distinct in various ways from the more universal versions/translations of the Bible used in other Christian religions, usually a King James version. All of this has seemingly resulted in some of the Catholic doctrines being divergent from those of other Christian religions.

For example, Catholic doctrine states that the mother of Jesus stayed a virgin, had no children by Joseph, and may have raised either Joseph's children from a previous marriage or some cousins of Jesus. Yet Matthew 1:25 in the Bible quotes God as stating that Joseph never "knew" Mary (the Biblical term for having sexual relations) until after the birth of her first- born son, and he called his name Jesus.

Another example of deviation from Biblical teaching is the practice of Catholics in "confession"—an act of telling one's sins privately to a priest to show repentance, with the priest then requiring the confessor to pray designated numbers of specific prayers as part of his/her penance for the sins. The priest acts as a mediator between God and the sinner, with the Catholic doctrine teaching that forgiveness is achieved by the sinner through the priest's intercession with God on the sinner's behalf. The priest, then, is a "middle-man" with God. In addition, receiving Holy Communion, an integral act in the Catholic religion, cannot occur in the church unless the recipient of such a holy ritual has gone to confession first and confessed his/her sins to a priest. Thus, the whole concept of God's forgiveness of our sins, once we individually repent of these, has been co-opted, for centuries, by priests and other Catholic clergy as middle-men. They have made themselves indispensable in our desire to be forgiven for our wrongdoing!

Finally, the Catholic Church is headed internationally by a Pope, as has been the case for many centuries, almost for the entire history of Catholicism. This Pope, who reigns like royalty until death, is surrounded by a hierarchy of priests, all male: bishops, archbishops, and cardinals, all of whom are invested with high levels of power, authority, and material well-being. Collectively, these highest-ranking clergy change the rules and institute new teachings in highly ritualized meetings in the Vatican. Fortunately, the present Pope Francis I, newly elected, appears to be deviating from many of these entrenched teachings and hierarchical dictums and placing a greater emphasis on true Christianity toward the poor and suffering, as Christ would do.

The Mormon Church

Most denominational churches have their own doctrines which are estranged in some way from the doctrine of Jesus. Just for example of a false prophet, Joseph Smith was the founder of the Church of Jesus Christ of the Latter Day Saints, known as the LDS church (The Mormons). The church was first organized in April 1830 just before the printing of the Book of Mormon, their version of a Bible. Allegedly this book provides additional revelations because the word of God depicted in the original bible had to be updated to restore the true meaning of the gospel. These revelations supposedly had been "hid up some fourteen hundred years," and an angel, named Maroni revealed to Joseph Smith the location in the State of New York where he was to dig. He finding "golden tablets," which the angel Maroni allegedly then gave him the power to decipher the hieroglyphics or unknown language on the tablets and is believed are the fundamentals on which the book of Mormon alters the gospel of Jesus is based, and a later publication titled *Doctrine and Covenants*.

The Mormon Church does not hide their belief that it is the only true church in the world. It believes that the apostle John is still alive today and this is based on *their* private interpretation of John 21 verses 21 through 23. They also have stated that the apostle regularly visits some elder in the church. The church was first organized early in 1830. It originally started with only six members. Today it is reported to be one of the fastest growing *religions* in the world. These two religions, Muslim and Mormon, effectively claim that the Bible is in error, that when Jesus cried out to God while on the Cross, "*It is finished*" that it was not finished. As a result of it not being finished Muhammad first and later Joseph Smith were allegedly anointed to correct the errors in the Bible made by Jesus, the prophets, Moses and the Apostles.

*   *   *

Both of these religions have succumbed to the "wiles" of our adversary, influencing and capturing the minds of the followers of these "religious "doctrines. There is, however, one great difference between Catholic and Mormon doctrines versus those of Islam: the two Christian religions reject violence and follow the doctrines of love and family, while Islam as expressed in the Qur'an and in the actions of Islamists embodies violence and never mentions "love."

I was born into a Mormon family and know that those who follow their doctrine obediently believe sincerely in many of the basic teachings of our Lord Jesus. However, both Islam and Mormon, although different, do not believe that Jesus was born of a virgin, or that our God fathered Jesus by His Holy Spirit overshadowing the Virgin Mary.

The Mormons believe that God is a man, that He has many wives, and that He materialized, took Mary as wife, and she bore His child Jesus as a natural event. The Muslims believe that Jesus was nothing more than a prophet of God and do not believe that Jesus went to the cross, died, shed His blood for the atonement of all sin for all people on earth, was resurrected, and is alive today.

When you think about these deviations from Christian belief, it is easy to recognize the fulfillment of Jesus' prophesies in Mathew 24:24. We must remember that Jesus gave us a new commandment, to "love one another as I have loved you." We have not been given a spirit to hate, or envy, nor have we been given the authority to judge any one. That is reserved for Jesus and Him alone. It is well to note that Matthew 13:49 states, "So shall it be at the end of the world the angels shall come forth, and sever the wicked from among the just."

There are, and have been, many false imitators of Christ and false prophets in this world and all seem to have their own code of belief and subsequent doctrine. They have all had one aim, even though unwittingly, and that is to "beguile" all who will seek, listen, and follow the true word of God. Matthew 24: 4, 23, 24 (KJV) describes Jesus teaching his disciples as follows: "Take heed that no man deceive you...for many shall come in my name, saying, I am Christ and shall deceive many.....Then if any man says unto you Lo, here is Christ, or there, believe it not. For there shall arise false Christs, and false prophets, and they shall show great signs and wonders, insomuch that if it were possible, they shall deceive the very elect." There are so many different sects under the name of religion throughout the world that all claim special communication with God. The word warns us to try the spirits, whether they are of God, and then tells us how to determine which are of God.

CHAPTER 6

The World Today

It appears that today, many children do not honor their parents, and in many families the parents do not honor their children. Neither do the parents raise their children in the ways of our Lord, or even tell them of Him. Worldly societies have for the most part aborted morality, and deny the sanctity of marriage, and by abortion have destroyed the sanctity of family values. Government has prohibited public schools to even mention the name Jesus, let alone opening class with a prayer. There is a great falling away from honoring God. True knowledge of Himself and Jesus generously made available by His grace has been taken away from the people of this world for centuries by Satan's influence.

God writes through His prophet Hosea, "My people are destroyed for lack of knowledge because you [the governments of leading nations] have rejected me. I will also reject you that you will be no servant to me, seeing that you have forgotten the law of your God, I will also forget your children" (Hosea 4:6). This was reiterated by Jesus in Luke 11:52 when He was addressing the Pharisees and Scribes concerning Mosaic Law, and He said to them: "Woe to you lawyers, [experts in law giving and enforcement] for you have taken away the key to knowledge." Reiterating this, Jesus, while being crucified, interceded for those who had participated in his crucifixion by asking His Father to "forgive them, for they know not what they do." Jesus thus specifically associated knowledge, or lack of knowledge, with ungodly behavior.

This is the same today in the entire world. Our ignorance of God and Jesus burdens all people as we have accepted ignorance (the lack of divine guidance), the knowledge of our God, and the

55

possibility of our receiving His promised lifestyle. This lack of knowledge prohibits our apprehensions of the instructions for living a righteous life. The gospel has been so badly compromised that religion today has been diluted by false prophets and teachers accepting degraded morals, which degrades the sanctity of marriage and family, denying prayer openly, and trying to organize a new world order that will have no room for God. This is not new, as I have noted above. Ever since the birth of evil and its expulsion out of heaven, it has been at work here to destroy all that God has wrought. Religion is one of the main targets of Satan, and he has progressively attacked religious practices through the vulnerable fallacy of man.

The Holy Spirit expressly says that in latter times, some will depart from the faith, giving heed to deceiving spirits and doctrines of demons, speaking lies in hypocrisy, having their own conscience seared with a hot iron (1 Timothy 4:1-2).

Studying God's promises we come to a prophetic promise of apostasy. Among those who are actually drifting into apostasy, this promise is certainly "unpopular." Additionally, in a church world that wrongly accepts what sounds positive and rejects what sounds negative (instead of rejecting error, and accepting truth), this promise is often met with disinterest or—worse!—disdain. "Faith" is the message of the word of God. It is the divine ultimate truth in which we are to place our faith, our trust. It especially includes the good news of the grace of our Lord Jesus Christ. Our present promise forewarns that there will be those who fall away from "the faith" as the days press closer and closer to the end of the church era. "In latter times some will depart from the faith." Since this is a departure, those who turn their backs on the word of God apparently had seemed to adhere to the word of God at some point. Then they turned away from it.

If the betrayers of Christianity remain active in the church world, their message will not be reflecting the true content of the scriptures. Peter gave a similar warning when he stated: "There were also false prophets among the people, even as there will be false teachers among you, who will secretly bring in destructive heresies, even denying the Lord who bought them" (2 Peter 2:1). As sure as

56

Israel had false prophets, the church will have false teachers. Paul provided some insights into their path of apostasy. They would be "giving heed to deceiving spirits and doctrines of demons." Giving credence to concepts that were perpetrated by demonic deception would result in errors in their doctrine. The devil and his army of evil spirits are intent on confusing and distorting the teaching of the word of God.

Typically, such errors feed man's fleshly desires to glorify the self. These apostates would also be "speaking lies in hypocrisy." Not only would their teaching be erroneous, their lives would be marked by falsehoods related to pretense. They would add untrue testimony to their inaccurate message. Perhaps the reports of their ministerial prowess would be grossly exaggerated. They would also be "having their own conscience seared with a hot iron." They would teach errors and live lies until their consciences were no longer convicted of sin. We are forewarned. Such apostates undoubtedly abound in these last days. I have to ask myself, does this satisfy the part in scripture that alludes to having one's name blotted out of the book of life?

This world today is wrought with many dangers as time comes to an end. Much confusion and frustration will reign; but if you know Jesus, He has told us to fear not, for He has promised (in Psalms 91:5-6) that we are protected against the darkness and violence that are to come.

It has been reported that ninety-four percent of students who have been raised with some church affiliation and go to college graduate not believing in God but in evolution. Only six out of a hundred return to church. Teaching Darwin's theory of evolution is a must while teaching religion, or even having a Bible in school, is prohibited. This is where we are today. Admittedly, there are those who will cite our U.S. Constitution with its "separation of church and state" provision. And there are also those who would say, "How would you like it if public schools required that Islam be taught in American schools, and that Islamic prayers [or Catholic, Buddhist, or Hopi prayers, etc.] should be recited in the classrooms?" This is indeed a question that divides our nation. Someone, somewhere will feel imposed upon, disrespected for his/her private beliefs, and marginalized. Is this fair? This is why our founding fathers insisted upon religion staying out of the public sphere.

We cannot ignore that the United States is highly diverse, and it thus includes every religion on earth: Christians, Buddhists, Jews, Muslims, Zoroasters, Hare Krishnas, just to name a few. When it comes to spiritual beliefs that fill people's hearts and guide them to be upstanding human beings and live an ethical life, there is no "one size fits all." The old proverb comes to mind: "Different strokes for different folks." Just as Muslims believe we Christians are on the wrong path, how just would it be to force American Muslims—or other believers—to follow just our Christian path?

So, what is the answer? Honoring the diversity of believers does not mean that we Christians cannot continue to disseminate the word of God and acknowledge the glory of God as widely as we can. Private citizens as well as "religious celebrities" like Billy Graham can continue to strengthen and expand their lifestyle and expressions of gospel dissemination. For example, let me tell you about the beautiful work of Chuck and Nancy Missler in their Koinonia House ("K-House," as we lovingly refer to it) ministry.

Chuck and Nancy reinvented themselves after a disastrous financial event destroyed their livelihood and material status, stripping away all they owned and leaving them destitute. Fortunately, the husband and wife team had always devoted significant time to their Christian involvements, through church and charity work, speaking, and writing. After the disaster that almost ruined them, the two decided to focus entirely on spreading the gospel of our Lord. They founded K-House, dedicated to creating and disseminating materials to help people learn and understand the teachings of the Bible. A nonprofit organization, K-House reached across the nation, other countries, and all cultures to spread the word of God. Chuck and Nancy have used in-depth teaching, writing books, speaking in radio interviews, going on lecture circuits, and developing a strong network of Christians serious about their study of scripture to help spread the gospel. If public schools cannot teach about the Bible, then it is up to us working in concert with one another to keep alive the word of God and strengthen it. There is strength in numbers.

These are challenging times, and they require clearly thought-out solutions to our concerns. Churches must become more active in their communities. Parents and other family members must find ways to connect with one another to share their love of Christianity and fill their children with this love. We Christians must, whenever appropriate, write letters to newspapers and other media to express our Christian values. More important, actions speak louder than words, and we must engage in charitable events whenever we can so others can see our love of our neighbors and caring for the vulnerable.

Unfortunately, some misguided "Christian" churches—like the Westboro Baptist Church, which has become known for staging funeral protests across our nation that mock the dead with slanders—have given the American public a skewed perception of what Christianity really represents. These "Christians" are not really Christians. They must be called to account by true Christians in America and denounced for their hate-mongering activities. Are leaders of such churches also "false prophets" that are misleading their congregations? Then legitimate Christian churches must come forward and set the record straight.

What happens to Christianity in today's turbulent times is in the hands of us Christians. We cannot change the Constitution or violate it, but we can take thoughtful, respectful, charitable actions to strengthen the ideals of Christianity across our nation.

The Best is Yet to Come

CHAPTER 7

Who Am I?

God tasked me to find, and understand, all I could about myself that I could then tell Him of my relationships I have with Him and with Satan. Psalms 51:5 tells me that I was conceived in my mother's womb in sin. Therefore, I began life as a child of the flesh, born with all sensual lusts controlled by my senses not yet having a purified heart, being born unto death as were all men after Adam, perhaps except those who were selected and predestined to be special envoys for the work of God (Ephesians 2:3; John 3:6; Romans 5:12).

Trying to recall any time or event when I became aware, or knowledgeable, that Jesus knew me and loved me, I drew a blank. I was born in my grandmother's home. She, with my grandfather, had migrated to America from Sweden after being converted by missionaries of the Mormon religion. They settled in Salt Lake City, Utah. My grandfather died three years before my birth. Grandmother was a devout church member, and a frequent attendee of the temple even at the age of 93, but I can't remember Mom or Dad ever attending their church services. I do remember that my mother dressed me for church one day, when I was about 6 years old, and sent me with two older brothers to attend Sunday services at our local ward house. After the praise with singing, I was sent with other young boys to a basement classroom for Sunday school.

I can't explain it, but I had a strong gut feeling at the time. I remember thinking, "I don't belong here." I felt out of place, detached. Was that a visitation from a ministering angel? I do not know. When I returned home my mother asked me, "How did you like church?" I told her what transpired, and she said that I would not have to attend again if that's how I felt about it. Perhaps that was a meaningful event.

61

My mother was an ardent Bible reader who also received a regular religious magazine titled *The Daily Word*. She would often read parts to me and taught me about Jesus, giving me a prayer of faith which has been part of my life ever since I was six years old.

I cannot honestly say that I knew Him even though I would pray that prayer of faith, and still do to this day. Not attending any church, I was not baptized until years later. Yet in the spring of 1945 I had a very definite visitation during a stressful event and heard audibly a very soothing voice telling me, "Fear not, for I am in control." The very next day my stressful issue had been resolved. I believe that was the moment I knew that He loved me. However, it was 24 years later that I was baptized in a Four-Square Church. The year was 1969, yet it took another 5 years before I relinquished all, including home, family, job, and my manner of life itself to God and Jesus for a more purposeful life.

Until that point in my life, I certainly could not think of any reason that God should love me. I was somewhat arrogant, self-centered, and had "married" my job at the expense of my family. Then one day, I was watching a program on television, broadcast by the Trinity Broadcasting Network, (TBN), when I decided to answer an invitation to make Jesus the Lord of my life. I was born again and became a new creature in Christ Jesus. It was the beginning of my new life, and just six years later, I lost my first wife to cancer. It was very difficult, and continues to be, to forgive myself for not protecting her from our adversary as I should have. I can relate to Adam and his spiritual challenges, but our merciful God did send to me in the coming years two other beautiful women that reflected His love for me.

Today I am writing about the end of this age, and the two ages to follow.

After the death of my first wife, I asked God why, while listening to the wee small voice of the Spirit of God. He expounded on the Excellency of the knowledge of our God and of Christ Jesus. The key to this knowledge was stolen or lost before the earthly ministry of Jesus by the malicious and devious work of Satan. He used the frailty of man's integrity, his egoism, pride, (self-exaltations), ignorance, and this world's political culture of legalism to take away the key (Luke 11:52). This condition has not changed to this day but has worsened. I knew that I could not write or say anything that God had not already written and thoroughly explained in His Word, but with His guidance compile in one document that which He engineered throughout the Bible to hide it from our adversary, Satan.

I asked myself often, why I am doing this? As I have previously stated, I can't add anything to what has already been expounded in His word; but, the Holy Spirit said, "Yes, but my children need the Key." Many have become victims of Satan's evil spirit and need enlightening and can relate to this story and be able to boldly apply the authority that I have given them in the name of Jesus to overcome the now powerless adversary. I still questioned my Lord, "Why me?" He told me that He chooses whomsoever He wills to be His servant, and that they are chosen even before they were substance in the womb, and the wages of sin passed on through birth is not imputed unto them, and then they are molded and shaped to serve Him. This is revealed in Isaiah 49:5, thus exposing an additional nature of God. He then suggested that I consider earlier servants like Abraham, Jacob, Joseph, all the prophets, and David. He then directed me to Psalms 138:8 where I heard Him say, "He will perfect that which concerns me and forsake not the works of my own hands." That finally did it, and I stopped asking Why me? I guess that I may be one of those "whomsoevers"; but, I know I have an intimate relationship with Him, and I intend to do whatsoever He instructs me to do. He then directed me to Romans 12:3, which reminded me that I should not think too highly of myself, and therein become a candidate to be snared by Satan's devilish temptations.

Yes, I now know who I am, and the awesome relationship and daily fellowship I have with my Father and Lord, and to Him belongs all accolades and Glory. I also know the undesirable influence Satan attempts so cunningly to have me manifest his deceitful lies in my life; but, by the power given me through the shed blood of Jesus, I now exercise authority over him, and give praises unto Jesus, and look

The Best is Yet to Come

forward to the day I stand before Him for judgment.

Franklin D. Murdock

CHAPTER 8

Our Greatest Menace

How many times have we heard the words, "The devil made me do it"? Many people worldwide carry a gun for personal protection, or to settle a dispute....even children. Prisons are full of inmates unable to overcome their anger, their personal lusts, immorality, self-destructive habits, and greed.

In His word we are instructed, "To be transformed from this world, and all its darkness to the light of His world by the renewing of our mind so that we may prove what is the good, and acceptable, and perfect will of God" so that we can become overcomers (Romans 12:1). We are exhorted to meditate on the words, "be transformed by the renewing of your mind." It becomes renewed by the power that is in your tongue, what you have in your heart, and the power we have in our tongue which we release by our spoken words and our communications. Jesus taught us to pray, and we finish our prayer with the word, "Amen," which means, "So be it." God has clearly shown us that this power we have in our spoken word can work negatively just as easily as it can work positively. It is your choice and my choice, each of us individually.

As it happened by the careless acts and the power of the spoken word by the anointed angel, God reveals it can happen to man. However, most of us never take the necessary time to seriously and diligently read our Father's intimate letter He wrote just for us personally. It contains all issues pertaining to our personal relationship with Him and each other. It is founded in love and is our trueness of life. Thus we never realize and consider the consequences of our actions, words spoken, and our attitude toward our spiritual well-being. Remember, as a man thinks in his heart, so is he. By the careless or evil words we speak, we not only bring disaster on us but we can be transformed into evil.

We don't need the devil Satan to do it. We do it ourselves. This is not to infer that Satan does not exist, but by our attitudes and selfness, we can make his work so much easier. To be an overcomer thus approved unto God and master evil we must first quench by mortifying that inherited sinful old man within us, and then accept by God's grace that new creature He plants in us with a heart of flesh and a new spirit at our rebirth.

I don't care how long you've been a believer or how long you've been practicing the principles of faith. You can easily slip into unbelief about the promises of God. And, when you do, it will cost you dearly. But if slipping into unbelief is so easy, you may say, "How can we avoid it?" Hebrews 4:11 tells us: "Let us labor therefore to enter into that rest, lest any man fall after the same example of unbelief." We must labor! Not by working with our hands and feet or struggling to get God to do something, but by spending time in God's word— hanging on to the promises of God by faith day after day. We must labor by hearkening to the Word and refusing to let it slip. Don't get casual, or lackadaisical about the Word. Don't make the mistake of thinking, Oh I know all that faith stuff. I hear it all the time being preached on television, and radio. It is well to note, there is a lot of difference between preaching and teaching. Don't slack off, because one of these days Satan will be able to influence your spirit; and through that relationship, he will catch you unprepared. So while you may think you are blessed, enjoying the amenities offered by living only in this world, Satan will steal you blind by taking from you your most precious possessions received from your loving Father.

Remember, the most powerful and mighty weapon made available to us is His word to master or rule over sin; but, it will do you no good if you don't know it, and the only way to know it is to study it to make yourselves approved unto God.

To use any other weapon is vanity.

CHAPTER 9

Where Are We?

I Peter 4:7 states: "The end of all things is at hand: be you therefore sober, and watch unto prayer." Yet some have the following philosophy:

Life is just a bowl of cherries. Happiness is where we find it, God helps those who help themselves, so let's make the most of it and we will have no sorrow. Go to school, get an education based on head knowledge, and make our mark in this world by self -sufficiency, and we will have no worries about tomorrow.

This is all a deceitful lie of Satan to which many of us may succumb. All is vanity and foolishness, for we as individuals become slaves to this kind of self-proclaimed dogma and become gullible subjects for Satan's deception. With an inflated ego and self-esteem, we feel comfortable concerning the passing of years and dream of our future retirement without fearful objection. If this is what we believe, the day will come when we will have a rude awakening to the absolute truths, and fall hard from our lofty perch. We may work hard, be good citizens, give to charities, support our alma mater, raise a family, and even go and tithe to church.

However, as the years have a way of passing quickly, there will come a time when our sight gets a little dimmer and our youthful prowess somehow goes astray. We will ponder our plight and begin the search for that which was always available had we only diligently studied to understand the spoken word of God and believed the teaching of Jesus and in Him trust and pray. Misleading and without truth, this self-righteous doctrine is supposing that material gain is Godliness and can produce contentment. However, Godliness with contentment is great gain for us to experience through an intimate fellowship and a commitment to our Lord Jesus, who said that we *all must* be born again in order for the Kingdom of God to enter. There is no other way under the canopy of heaven that any works that man can do will render the same results.

As we all must someday say good-bye to loved ones and leave this, our temple of clay, we shall find the truth in the title *The Best Is Yet to Come,* as all promises become unmistakably true. It is written, "When He, the Spirit of truth, has come, He will guide you into all the truth. He will glorify me, for He will take of what is mine and declare it to you." Now we have received the Spirit who is from God, that we might know the things that have been freely given to us by God.

Where Am I?

So where are we? First ask yourself, Where am I? Having lived on this planet earth, which has become such a messed up world, for more than 90 years, I have to ask: How come, and what is the reason, and is there a purpose? So I asked God to please explain. I asked Him this: Why did you create all this mess? Why? He answered by divine revelation through His word and anointed messengers, and this is what I heard:

The first thing I had to deal with is the iniquity that had become evident in my anointed cherub that evolved into an evil force, which caused great discord, and that I could not tolerate in any way within my kingdom. I had to identify the cause then establish a plan of action that would assure a total eradication of that iniquity, which is the cause of what you call 'mess,' and

69

the potential of it ever recurring. When my cherished and anointed angel became muteness, and became such a discord in my abode, my most high secret place, the first requirement was, I had to have a place, other than heaven, where I could oversee and control everything until my plan could come to the required completion. So I created the earth and all associated heavens to provide a place for the temporary incarceration of Satan and his follower angels. This was necessary until I could prepare a place where they could be eternally confined, and from which there could be no escape. You must realize that he and the angels that followed him have eternal life, and cannot be exterminated or just die and be returned to that from which he comes, as is mortal man.

The voice spoke clearly to me, and expressed needs that I, as a mortal, could understand and relate to. Point by point, the Lord explained to my spirit how and why our world and our earthly lives had evolved as they had.

God's Explanations for Our Earthly Woes

The Lord opened my eyes to see his love and concern for us, which was being challenged by the evil that had entered our earthly planet and heavens. This is what He said:

- "I needed a companion, a co-worker or co-laborer, a confidante that would be part of me and would assist me, so I created man in the exact image of myself, and having all likenesses of my nature and character, and would share with me the power of my Spirit, but would for a time he created a little lower than my angels, being mortal."
- "Before I could accept my created man as an integral part of me, and therefore becoming family, he would

have to voluntarily overcome the inherent fallacy, the iniquity that was inherited from Adam who had succumbed to Satan's deceptive lies."

- "For me to make the change of design of my created man, or do for him a permanent change of his character, and it not be necessary for him to choose would have made man in the fashion of a robot, or puppet with strings attached, and therefore not after my likeness. However, I have provided the sufficiency through the blood of Jesus for him to overcome this fallacy of character within him, and to overcome all evil associated with this world."

- "Satan, the Devil, had to be removed from my abode, Heaven, so he was expelled from his high place of responsibility in my high and mighty abode, and ejected to earth and its heavens. I then forewarned all that lived on the earth of the danger they were in, due to them now being exposed to Satan who is very angry, and that terror would come on earth, its heavens, and seas."

- "The purpose and goal I have is as follows: Completely eradicate any discord, and the cause of self-exaltations by anyone within the realm of my kingdom, and reconcile between me and man the oneness of spirit.

- "So what you call 'mess' is all the actions from a very angry and deceitful adversary who, knowing the appointed time of his demise is at hand, is very active."

- "All the destructive catastrophes experienced by this world are the results of his anger due to his travail. They will all be quieted with my return. But before my return, the following, as it is written, must come to pass."

- "I will remove the Holy Spirit and call my church from all the earth."

- "The world governments will economically collapse giving cause for man to be delusional, and believe lies."

- "The anti-Christ will be identified, and he will establish the predicted one world government, and religion with a false peace for a period."
- "There will be a time of great confusion, and there will be much anguish with famines, food shortages, and lack of love or concern for one another among the nations, and tribes as they will fight for what they conceive as their survival
- "The return of your Lord Jesus at the end of the seven years will mark the   end of this age, the age of dispensation of grace, and to establish His everlasting kingdom here on earth with a multitude of saints to serve and reign with Him."
- "There will begin a period wherein all truths shall be revealed, and the final separating of those who insist on retaining their attitude of selfness before final judgment is to be rendered. Jesus paid the ransom for the redemption of all that would believe, but these are those who choose to retain an attitude of 'me first,' or 'I must be in control,' which is unbelief."
- "Then, the best that has been saved will become reality, and all those who have been redeemed, and sanctified, made Holy, will inherit with Jesus all that I have built up for this appointed time, and will inhabit the refined and cleansed earth and new heavens for eternity."

I was stunned. I must admit that I did not know what to expect, but was not surprised. I had not heard anyone teach this, and wondered who else may have received such a revelation, or was I a chosen vessel to announce this for all believers to relish, for it is written, the best is saved for last.

Jesus taught the disciples and those within hearing range in parables. They are as applicable today, or perhaps more, as they were the day he taught them. For should you realize the meaning of the word *disciple*, you would know it means *learner, follower, or student*, and that describes you and me, as each day we seek to find God's truths, we are believing learners and therefore are disciples. I am not going to literally review each parable because I know you have either read them or heard them. But, like me, you probably apprehended them as comparative stories for the listeners only of the day of the ministry of Jesus; but those parables define the Kingdom of Heaven, and it is important you keep this in mind, for they define your destined future home.

I highly recommend you read them again in light of what was revealed to me by God, and I have relayed to you above. I emphasize very strongly that these parables are in the scripture for you and me today. I ask you, does God keep secrets from us? Yes, indeed, God's word informs us, that it might be fulfilled, which was spoken by the prophet, saying I will open my mouth in parables. I will utter things which have been kept in secret from the foundation of the world. Remember, Satan is described as the sum of all wisdom, and God so engineered the scripture to keep from him knowledge of His master plan.

You may ask how this is applicable to us today. Read very thoughtfully in Matthew 35: 47-49. They compare these parables to the gathering of his church into the kingdom of heaven using a fisherman's net. After the net is drawn in, Angels of the Lord separate the good from evil, the righteous from the unrighteous, and the wicked from the just. As you can see, this is yet to happen, and we should judge ourselves to determine just where we personally are in the master plan of God, as it pertains to our being approved unto God, and then be accepted into His Kingdom.

Problems in Our World Today

The Best is Yet to Come

To realize where mankind is collectively, just turn on
the news on the radio or television, and you will be bombarded
with political rhetoric filled with worldwide legalisms and
geopolitical correctness. This chaotic rhetoric is tied to huge
social changes to all societies, and to so-called natural
disasters like earthquakes, volcano eruptions, uncontrolled,
manmade ecological poisoning of this world's seas, lakes, and
rivers, poisoning which destroys our primary food sources. The
ecological disasters alone lead to massive economic failures
and loss of trust in those who supposedly lead the populace.
These world events, both physical and political, confirm
Biblical prophecies predicting religious apathy and the end of
this age, the age of grace. Accordingly, I believe we are now in
the last days of this age and nearing the end of times.

Believing the word of God, I am witnessing men of all
nations becoming confused and seemingly lacking visionary
leadership as trouble increases. There is a falling away from
truth with men denying God. During a teaching session
described in the Bible, Jesus said that as it was in the days of
Noah, so shall it also be in the days of the Son of Man. In
Noah's time the inhabitants of earth were eating, drinking, and
marrying without reverence. In the days of Lot, people were
doing the same; but the same day that Lot left Sodom, fire and
brimstone from heaven destroyed all. As it was before, it is the
same today, and men are not receiving the love of the truth,
that they might be saved. God shall thus soon be sending, and
may have already sent, the inhabitants of this earth a strong
delusion that they all might be damned, in order that the
inhabitants of earth are programmed to receive the Son of
Perdition, a person with a glib manner of communication to
deceive all people alive on earth at that time to believe this lie.

This may be difficult to comprehend, that God, who is
love, would do such a thing. But God has continually warned
us that there is a limit to His patience. God will remove His
Church and His Holy Spirit from this earth, allowing free reign

74

to Satan for   pouring out His wrath as prophesied, known as
the period of tribulation. Jesus will come to gather His Saints
to be with Him (an event known in the Bible as "the rapture").
This escape, or protection from imminent evil, was predicted
even before Jesus was manifested in this world. Here, He
exposed his true character to protect his faithful followers from
evil.

Read very carefully each prophetic word recorded in scriptures,
for they reveal God's judgment and God's mercies, twin themes of the
prophets describing the destruction that will impact the earth in the day
of God's judgmental wrath to clean-up this world's mess. The last day
is also the day of redemption of the remnant of His chosen. As you
read ancient prophecies, keep in mind that in order for the early
prophecies to be fulfilled, it was imperative that two conditions on
earth had to first be manifest. They were as follows: (1) Israel had to
be a nation in the land granted by God to their fathers, and (2) Israel
had to be in control of Jerusalem. The first happened in May, 1948,
and the second after the six-day war in 1967. So the conditions are
now in place.

While researching scriptures I found the following dissertation
related directly to the validity of God's word being an absolute, and
pass it on for your edification:

Herodotus, an ancient Greek historian who lived in the 5th
century B.C.E., is regarded as the "Father of History" in Western
culture. He wrote: "The history of Tyre, also known as Tyrus,   began
2750 B.C. It was a fortified City in Joshua's time and later became a
great maritime commercial center. The prophets Isaiah, Jeremiah, and
Ezekiel foretold of the utter destruction for Tyre, naming not less than
25 separate details each of which during the following centuries came
true literally. Mathematicians have estimated, according to the law of
Compound Probabilities, that if a prophecy concerning a person, place,
or event has 25 details beyond the possibility of human collusion,
calculation, coincidence, and comprehension, there is only 1 chance in
more than 33.5 million of it [being an] accidental fulfillment. Yet
Tyre's history under the hands of Nebuchadnezzar, and then more than

two centuries later at the hands of Alexander the Great, and Centuries after that at the hands of the crusaders, was the striking fulfillment of the prophets' forecasts. No other city in the world's history could have fulfilled them. The authenticity and creditability of God's word leaves no chance for sane denial."

I add the God-breathed word is an absolute truth, just as Jesus proclaimed.

So, where are we? It is evident that we are now in a period of time denoted as the end of this age, the age of Jesus completing what He declared in Matthew 16:18 that, upon the rock of truth, He would build His church and the gates of hell shall not prevail against it. We are experiencing the last calling before he calls his bride home and shuts the door. So where are we in relation to God's appointed time? While writing this saga I have many times apprehended His presence with guidance and I want to share His love. He has told me to be diligent and to be prepared for His visitation to remove His church, and has provided adequate descriptions of signs that will foretell the season of the end. In addition to watching your favorite athletic team at play, or what is shaping up to be a challenging political battle in the next national election cycle, it will be most rewarding for you to seriously study and apply God's instructions, that you may be accepted unto His promised eternity.

Franklin D. Murdock

CHAPTER 10

The Rapture

It is with some concern that I find many Christians today thinking the declaration that Jesus made when He said, "I will come to receive you" is not a statement of truth. But God cannot lie, and there is nothing too difficult for Him. He was speaking to all believers, obedient doers of His word, His church. Jesus was referring to gathering up the faithful to Him so they would escape the wrath of God, called the rapture, in the endtimes. My concern is that many people—including pastors, evangelists, TV preachers, and others of varying religious affiliations—do not believe that Jesus will do this. But this rejection of Jesus' claim that He will return was prophesied by the Apostle Peter, who stated that even persons dedicated to religious work as their calling would negate the idea that Jesus Christ would be returning to earth (2 Peter 3:3-8).

God's return in the rapture is an ancient prophecy, as discussed in a prior chapter of this book. Perhaps because the Jews were exiled and scattered throughout the world for more than 1,750 years before being miraculously brought back by God in 1948 never to be scattered again (Jeremiah 30:3 and Ezekiel 46:18), many people of the world became accustomed to believing that the ancient prophecy of the rapture could never happen because the two Biblical conditions for it to occur (Jews having their own homeland and being in control of Jerusalem) were so unthinkable and seemingly impossible.

Comprehending that there ever could be an established Jewish nation amongst Israel's staunch, bitter enemies in the Middle East was a difficult feat for anybody. Yet, against all odds, today Israel miraculously exists as a sovereign nation and is indeed in control of Jerusalem. It is alarming that many nations of the world are aligned against this very small country, but this is in accord with prophesied scripture. Also, there are those who want to divide their God-given homeland, and even the holy City of God, Jerusalem, among nomads, which will not happen.

For all people who have relinquished all selfness to Jesus and are overcomers by their trust in God, the rapture is a blessing, and in accordance with that written in Luke 21: May we be accounted worthy to escape all wrath of the tribulation, to stand face to face with the son of man. I have stated previously that we are to master, or rule over, Satan and sin. As I study the word I understand that the rapture will reveal whether or not we, as God's helpers, have built our lives on His precepts and instructions. (Read very carefully 1Corithians 3:8-15.) All who have received Jesus will be saved but some will receive awards. If any of you have failed to heed God's instructions, learn and apply them as quickly, for God's word is truth and is an absolute. The calling-up, or rapture, of all His church in heaven, asleep in Christ, and those alive at the time, will first assemble together in the clouds with Jesus, then assemble in heaven with earlier saints and an innumerable company of angels.

Hebrews 12:22-24 presents a compelling picture of the rapture. Experiencing the rapture is the beginning again, and after the rapture, you will be groomed in fine linen for the wedding supper of the Lamb, for we are the bride of Christ. (Revelation 19:7-9 also helps us picture the rapture.) We then shall prepare for the next age, the post tribulation period known as the Millennial Age, wherein Jesus will reign as King of Kings and Lord of Lords for a thousand years, and we will return to earth with Him to be His servants and reign with Him. Yes, the rapture by any other name—e.g., catching up, calling up, or removal of His saints—is all the same, and as prophesied, it will come to pass.

My Vantage Point as an Older Christian

I am over 90 years old, and handicapped, being deemed legally blind. I have two mechanical heart valves and a pacemaker. I am a veteran of World War II and have seen what violence on a large scale can and does do to human beings. I have suffered the deaths of three wives in my long life. But I am blessed to live a fulfilling, productive life in a retirement and assisted living establishment. I see the blessings and goodness of God all around me yet am still amazed at the seeming apathy and lack of spiritual awareness in many people with whom I interact. When I bring up the subject of the rapture for friendly discussion, I receive responses that are appalling, such as the following:

- God don't want me to worry about that. That is God's problem, not mine.

- I don't know about those things. People have taught this for a thousand years, and nobody knows anything about it. It is a secret known only to God, so don't even try to tell me anything about it.

- They are over my head, so I leave all that to my church leaders about the rapture.

- No, I believe we will have to go through the tribulation to be witnesses for God.

For the most part, both my fellow residents and facility staff members have an attitude of apathy or lack of any personal responsibility for maneuvering their lives through the maze of what they call nature. They say such things as God is responsible for all things that happen. It is not difficult for me to apprehend, for it wasn't too long ago that I, too, lacked the knowledge of divine truths. But I found in 1 John 2:27 that I needed no man to teach me. It was then that God began molding and shaping me into what I am today. Yet, things did not change overnight. It required a lot of soul-searching and confessing to my heavenly Father my sins against Him before I meet Him, my Abba Father, to consummate an intimate relationship with Him.

Throughout the scripture we are forewarned to be prepared and watchful, not be complacent. The visitation of our Lord to claim His bride, the church that He has built, for if we over-occupy our minds with worldly matters, we may miss His visitation, as did the five virgins in the parable of the ten virgins, for we know not the day or hour of His visitation. But Jesus taught much about recognizing the season and thus being prepared.

Quoting 1 Corinthians 2:16: "For who has known or understood the mind (the counsels and purposes) of the Lord so as to guide and instruct Him and give him knowledge? But we have the mind of Christ, the Messiah, and do hold the thoughts (feelings and purposes) of His heart." In Matthew 6:33 Jesus directs us to first seek the Kingdom of God and all its righteousness. Luke 17:21 informs us not to look elsewhere for the Kingdom because the Kingdom of God is within us. The key is to seek diligently and continually for, by our seeking, we shall find what we seek, as Jesus proclaimed in Matthew 7:7.

Isn't it exciting to realize that we can hold the thoughts and feelings and purposes of God's very own heart in our heart? Isn't it thrilling to know the Creator of heaven and earth will be one spirit with us and transmit His thoughts to our mind? In 1 Corinthians 6:17 it says that when we were joined to the Lord, we became one spirit with Him. He came into union with man so that He can talk to us heart-to-heart. God wants each of us in harmony with Him so that His thoughts can become our actions. He wants us to walk so closely with Him that we never lack power to overcome the evil of this world until we experience the rapture.

He wants us to be so in tune with His Spirit, that we are able to feel His heart of compassion toward those among us who are burdened with ignorance and lack of knowledge. He wants to be one with you and me, so He can reach out through our hands and fulfill His purposes on this earth. Make a fresh commitment today to walk in union with our God. Give your attention to His Spirit in your inner man. Determine to yield to His voice and not to the voices of the world or the flesh! Allow the mind of Christ to flow through you! Let not any temporary situation or stress master you, for Jesus said, whatever I have done, you will also do but even more. I say to you, do not allow any thought that does not edify your knowledge of God and Jesus, you or your heavenly family, or your life with Jesus.

I am legally blind, yet today I see more clearly the Glory of God than I was able to see a few years ago, and I hear His voice speaking to my heart every day. What I have written is what He revealed to me in answer to my inquisitive questions while in prayer.

Franklin D. Murdock

CHAPTER 11

The Antichrist, Son of Perdition

Jesus said, "As it was in the days of Noe (Noah), so shall it be also in the days of the Son of Man" (Matthew 24:37). This alludes basically to two conditions, both of which are not good news for most of humanity, as follows:

1. That man will be so disconnected from the word of God and so disillusioned, he will not be aware what is really happening, as the people of Noah's day were caught unaware when the flood struck.

2. Evil had engulfed the people so much, that it grieved God to the extent He was prepared to destroy everyone.

This chapter discusses the suffering which will be part of the endtimes, including the manifestation of the Antichrist, the Son of Perdition, as prophesied in Revelations. This coming tribulation, the manifestation of the Antichrist, will have great anguish and consequences, until the Antichrist is defeated by God.

Take a moment and think of the anguish and pain suffered by the Jews through the multiple holocausts to which they have been exposed throughout much of recorded history. This evil against people on a large scale is at work today and will culminate with the destruction of one-fourth of all humanity alive at that day before Jesus returns to salvage the remnants of His family. According to the Bible, there are four major events that will occur sequentially, as follows:

84

1. The rapture will occur in which the true church of Jesus Christ and the Holy Spirit are taken by God from this earth, thus leaving much confusion throughout the world.

2. A man capable of falsely displaying himself as a man of vision will be acknowledged and selected by a body of nations to hopefully lead the world to economic stability.

3. Finally, this man will bring the hostile nations to a peace agreement, and he will assume the position of dictator over this new worldwide order.

4. This Antichrist will eventually require people to take his mark on their right hand or their forehead (Revelation 13:11-17) to be able to survive economically, eventually dooming these followers to destruction by God, and eventually bringing about his own destruction by Jesus Christ.

This Antichrist, the Son of Perdition, will be working under the auspices and direction of Satan. Don't confuse this agent of evil with the multitudes of anti-Christs, or anti-religious elements, prevalent today and throughout recorded history. God reveals in 2 Thessalonians 2:2-8 what will happen before the Son of Perdition is revealed. Verse 7 states: "This lawlessness is already at work secretly, and it will remain secret until the one who is holding it back steps out of the way." Verse 8 says: "Then the man of lawlessness will be revealed." That something that must be removed is the church and Holy Spirit that abides in each faithful believer.

The Antichrist is the embodiment of evil, in opposition to Christ, who is the embodiment of love. The Antichrist attempts to rule the world in place of the Lord, and he is described thus: "He opposes and exalts himself above every so-called god or object of worship, so that he takes his seat in the temple of God, declaring himself to be God" (2 Thessalonians 2:1-4 NRSV, 1989).

As prominent Biblical scholar and author Chuck Missler wrote in his article, "Mischievous Angels or Sethites?," in his *Personal Updates* in 1997, the similarity between the endtimes and the ancient flood of Noah's time is an important one to apprehend. Missler states: "The unique events leading to the Flood are a prerequisite to understanding the prophetic implications of our Lord's predictions regarding His Second Coming."[1]

Regarding both the deluge in Noah's time and the suffering to come in the endtimes, God inflicted, and will again inflict, His wrath upon mankind for its sinfulness and departure from His word. In both cases, it will be a case of the world became too filled with evil, and a fresh start toward the kingdom of God was, and will be, needed. In a second article, "The Return of the Nephilim?" (which is actually Part Two of the article cited above), also in 1997, Chuck Missler described how the endtimes would look, as depicted in Luke 21:25-26: "And there shall be signs in the sun, and in the moon, and in the stars; and upon the earth distress of nations, with perplexity, the sea and the waves roaring, Men's hearts failing them for fear and for looking after those things which are coming on the earth for the powers of heaven shall be shaken." Again, as in Noah's time, there is great flooding, fear, and destruction across the world.

Connected to this endtimes scourge will be the ascension and prominence of the Antichrist on the world stage after the rapture and the suffering he will bring. According to some, the Antichrist will be a person who is highly persuasive and presents himself as a man of peace, thus attracting followers. He may actually, at first, help the world attain peace on some fronts; but some Biblical scholars and others believe that the Antichrist will be a human being with Satan "indwelling" within him, and with Satan's power through the Antichrist being lesser than that of God.[2] Divinity professor Bernard McGinn explains the Antichrist as follows:

"For Christians, God is the creator of all things, including Satan and the Antichrist. In so far as they are creatures, they come from God, and their being is a being that was given to them by the goodness of the Creator.... Evil demonstrates the mystery of free will, both in an angelic creature like Satan, and in a human being like the Antichrist.

Although Satan and the Antichrist set themselves up against God through the exercise of their freedom, they are part of a divine plan, according to apocalyptic belief." [3]

In this divine plan, Jesus Christ will prevail over the Antichrist, destroying him with a breath (2 Thessalonians 2:7-10) and casting him into the lake of fire and sulfur (Revelation 20:10) for eternal damnation.

I must ask: Are we all ready for the endtimes, and would we be able to resist the Antichrist's wiles and remain steadfast in our adherence to God's word?

---

[1] Matthew 24:37.

[2] Cabinet, Kristofer Widholm, and Bernard McGinn (2001). "Antichrist: An Interview with

Bernard McGinn." In

http://www.cabinetmagazine.org/issues/5/widholm.php

[3] Ibid.

CHAPTER 12

Re-Establishing Relationship

The establishment of God's heavenly Kingdom on this earth is the beginning of a new age known as the Millennial Age. It will begin after the return of Jesus to this earth with his army of saints as his servants and helpers when He puts an end to the time of tribulation and imprisons Satan in the bottomless pit where he will stay for a thousand years. Those alive on this earth will be separated as just or unjust.

Remember, there will be more than 4.5 billion souls inhabiting this earth when Jesus returns and before He begins to establish His Kingdom after the 7 years of tribulation. First, this number will be reduced by an unknown quantity totaling all who have believed the great lie of the Antichrist and worshipped the beast or his image and received his mark on their forehead or hand. They will all be slain and their carcasses fed to the vultures of the air (Revelation 19:17-18). Second, the number will be further reduced as Jesus will send forth His angels to separate the *tares* (*weeds*, meaning the children of iniquity). They will be separated from the wheat, (those who are seen as righteous), and will be burned in the fire, as He stated in the parable of a man that sowed good seed (which is the word of God) in his field, and the devil came afterward and planted weeds among the good seed (Matthew 13:24-42, KJV).

I think it most important to recognize that this is talking of the end of this age in which we now live, sometimes referred to as the end of this world, as Jesus referred to it in Matthew, verse 40, as he said, "Just as the weeds are sorted out and burned in the fire, so it will be at the end of the world." I quote the words spoken by Jesus to his disciples in verses 41 and 42: "The son of man shall send forth his angels, and they shall gather out of his kingdom all things that offend, and them which do iniquity; and shall cast them into a furnace of fire: There shall be wailing and gnashing of teeth."

As it is today, there are many *tares* throughout this world, including false religious dogmas and doctrines along with many nonbelievers that will first be judged and be cast out, reducing the number of souls that will enter His Kingdom. As Jesus said in Matthew 13:43: "Then shall the righteous shine forth." It is after these events have been accomplished that Jesus will begin His reign as King and establish His eternal kingdom on earth, "as is in Heaven," according to the Lord's Prayer.

The first order of business will be to restore the intimate relationship that first existed between God and Adam with His new family. He will reign as king over all the nations and their inhabitants of the earth for one thousand years from the throne of David. There will no longer be a government for the people and by the people as we know it today. He will have total power and authority. No one can protest His actions or decisions. He will have the help of many saints that will reign with him as his servants and priests.

The truth and reason for this millennial period of time is clearly defined in God's written word, however very majestically and cleverly concealed from all who have their minds blinded by the god of this world. The following is only an introduction to a more encompassing picture or definition of all that must be transformed from this material world to our new, perfected spiritual world.

The Holy Spirit of God led and influenced me to write the following: First and foremost this carnal world on this planet earth has no relevant relation with the world known as heaven in God's eternity, which will also prevail here on earth after this Millennial Age. This should be everyone's hope of all glory to be approved unto God to advance into this glorious and exceedingly final home with God and Jesus. All inhabitants of this carnal world have been programmed to consider events that happen here as natural events; and when God performs something unexplainable, we call it "supernatural" and "a miracle." But that is simply because we are ignorant of the true precepts that prevail in God's world. Yet these precepts have always been required of all God's children to know and obey because they will apply to this world during the reign of Jesus, and become permanent thereafter.

It is most important that you realize that they have to be understood and followed to the letter, or you will not develop the faith required to be approved by God to inherit the glorious future that God promises when this earth is refreshed and renewed. Before entering God's final age of eternity, all this must be individually accomplished. The alternative of this is eternity in the lake of fire with Satan, the fallen angels and false prophets, and all that refused God and Jesus. Those who are left in the Millenial Age might total fewer than what man's religions teach, and all will require being re-educated to understand God's precepts and forget unwanted religious and scientific technological rudiments associated with this present world.

There are many examples given us throughout the Bible to prepare us for the changes predicted, and each of them contains a specific message. I will use only four specific examples to define your basic responsibility to comply with God's master plan to re-establish man's relationship with God, as God had with Adam before the precious relationship was destroyed.

Four Paradigms for God's Master Plan

Paradigm 1: Knowledge with Understanding

Jesus makes it clear in Luke 14:36 where He said while addressing a crowd of followers: "If any man come to me and hates not his father, and mother, and wife, and children, and brothers, and sisters, yea, and his own life also, he cannot be my disciple." This may be difficult to understand, especially because God had written a commandment in stone that man should honor his father and mother, and later Jesus gave a new commandment that man love one another as He loved each of you.

90

This all sounds like a contradiction, but in truth it is not. It is really emphasizing the intimate relationship that God requires we have with Him. Luke 14:36 could have been stated as follows: "If any man wants or desires to follow me and be a disciple of mine, he must love me first, and love less his father, mother, wife, children, brethren, sisters, and even his own life." One meaning of the word "hate" as used in Luke 14:36, according to a Greek dictionary, is "loves less." This is why it is so important to study the word, and not just read or listen to it. This type of love relationship is emphasized throughout both the Old and New Testaments.

Paradigm 2: Honor and Commitment

In Judges 11, God's word informs us of the story of a man named Jephthah who was fathered by Gilead, but whose mother was a prostitute. Gilead and his wife raised him along with many other children of their own. Jephthah grew to be a great warrior and a man of valor. After the death of his father Gilead, Jephthah, having a family of his own, was expelled from his home by his half-brothers and sisters because he was born of a strange woman and they did not want him to inherit any of their father's land. He, with his family, fled and lived among strangers where he had no friends of character.

Time passed, and when the Amorites began their war against Israel, the elders of Gilead sent for Jephthah to return and be their commander and help them fight the Amorites to retain their lands. After much conversation of things past and after his half-brothers agreed that he would be the head of their house, he agreed, and returned to command the army of Israel. During the course of battles, in prayer asking the Lord to deliver the Amorites into his hands, he made a vow unto the Lord. He said: "If You, without fail, deliver the children of Amon into my hands, then it shall be, that whatsoever cometh forth of the doors of my house to meet me, when I return in peace from the children of Ammon, shall surely be the Lord's, and I will offer it up for a burnt offering."

I have struggled to grasp the meaning of God's message in this scripture, but by His grace, God has revealed a mystery not yet understood by man and therefore is not being taught by religious teachers. It has to do with the most important commandment given to man, which is: "Love thy Lord God with all your heart, with all your soul, and with your entire mind." Keep this in mind as I complete the story of Jephthah, and feel the agony he must have had when he returned to his home.

The first thing that emerged through the door of his home was his only child, a 17-year- old daughter. As she came out to meet him playing a tambourine and dancing for joy, he tore his clothing in deep anguish. As she greeted him he cried out, "Oh, my daughter you have completely destroyed me! You have brought disaster on me! For I have made a vow to the Lord, and I cannot take it back." Her reply was a reflection of total compliance with the commandment to "honor your father and mother" when she replied, "Father, if you have made a vow to the Lord, you must do to me what you have vowed, for the Lord has given you a great victory over your enemies, the Amorites. But first let me go up and roam in the hills and weep with my friends for two months, because I die a virgin." He granted her the two months she requested. When she returned, he kept his vow that he had made to the Lord, and his daughter died a virgin.

The deep and comprehensive message our father intends for His children to understand may not be totally manifest until Jesus establishes His Kingdom during His millennial reign. Yet it exemplifies the necessity to be obedient even to the words you speak, honoring your commitments and vows. To really comprehend and understand the power we have in our tongue and the spoken word is one important value we must learn, and not use vain or careless verbal expressions.

Paradigm 3: Faith and Trust

The message relates to Abram, later changed by God to Abraham, and his transformation from idolatry. It was 292 years after the flood when Abram was born a seventh-generation descendant of Shem, a son of Noah, and was the youngest of three sons of Terah living at the time in the city of Ur. Abram married Sarai. Later when Abram's brother, who had fathered a boy child named Lot, died, his father brought the child to Abram and Sarai to care for him. His father decided to move this family to the land of Canaan, but stopped at a place called Haran in the land of Mesopotamia and dwelt there.

Abram and his father's house had no personal relationship or fellowship with God, for their ancestors from Shem until Abram had drifted into idolatry, worshiping lesser gods. This changed when Abram received a visit by God. In Haran, God visited Abram and identified Himself saying, "I am your Lord God and you are to leave your native land, your country, and from your kindred, and from your father's house, unto a land that I will show you: And I will make of you a great nation, and I will bless you, and make your name great; and you shall be a blessing: And I will bless them that bless you, and curse him that curses you: and in you all families of the earth [will] be blessed."

This is a unilaterally made covenant between God and Abraham. At this time nothing was expected, or demanded, of Abraham except he follow God's instructions which constituted the new beginning of God's plan to restore the lost relationship between Him our Father and His created man.

Abram's wife Sarai was barren and could not provide Abraham a son through which future generations could materialize, yet God had promised Abraham he would have heirs. It may baffle men when they realize God's timing is not theirs. God is not slow, or late. He is always on time, so when His promises are manifest, you will know they are from Him. Abraham and Sarai had waited 25 years before Sarai conceived at the age of 90 years and gave Abraham, who was then 100 years old, their son Isaac.

There is so much in the life of Abraham that contains messages for us today pertaining to life and God's overall plan, but I want to focus on only one. That is when Isaac was grown into a young lad, and miraculous things transpired before and after his birth. Now God tempted Abraham's faith by saying to him, "Take your son Isaac, whom you love so much, and go to the land of Mariah. There offer him as a burnt offering, on one of the mountains which I will show you."

Because of the limited true spiritual knowledge and comprehension of the true love and nature of God, and my Lord Jesus, I have difficulty imagining the thoughts that were Abraham's. Yet he complied totally, and was at the point of plunging a knife into the lad to kill him as Isaac lay bound on a sacrificial altar. Then, at the last moment, an angel of the Lord stopped him, saying, "Don't lay a hand on the boy." Then said the angel, "Do not hurt him in any way, for now I know you truly fear God and that you have not withheld from me even your son, your only son."

Then suddenly behind Abraham was a ram with its horns caught in a bush. Abraham then slew and offered that ram as a burnt offering unto God. He then named the place "Jehova-Jireh, which means, "The Lord will provide."

Subsequently God spoke to Abraham again and said, because you have shown me your faith in my word I will swear unto myself that I will in blessing, [certainly] bless you, and I will multiply your seed [descendants] as the stars of the heaven, and as the sand which is upon the seashore; and your seed shall possess the gate of his enemies; And through all your seed shall all the nations of the earth be blessed." Thus it is that the Lord later explained through the writings of Paul that if we be Christ's (that is, if we abide in Him and His word abides in us), we are the seed of Abraham.

It is difficult to comprehend with understanding the stern love of God who mandates that His children love Him intimately, and above all else even unto death. This appears to the carnal-minded, earthbound man having the experience of struggling to make ends meet in today's hectic, advanced society as something beyond reality. It is nothing more that utter confusion. This world is evil, influenced by the god of this world, and man has allowed the knowledge of this world to harden his heart, thus blocking the thoughts God sends toward us, by grace with a predicted end (Jeremiah 29:11-12). This disconnect with God's word makes it difficult for us to practice faith and trust in the Lord, which are paramount.

Paradigm 4: Jesus as the Perfect Example of Commitment and Obedience

When that treasonous anointed Cherub that was God's covering angel became transformed through his greed for power into the devil Satan, God put into action His master plan to subdue and annihilate him forever, and at the same time establish His Kingdom on an earth united in total love. To initiate this plan God needed someone to represent Him in such a manner that His true will could not be denied. There was no angel in heaven that could perform the needed task, so He had to come in the form of man himself. God created a live embryo of Himself and used His Holy Spirit to implant it in the womb of the Virgin Mary. In today's technology you might say He cloned himself and, using the female version of man, created "the son of man." Yet this embryo was the son of God, Jesus. Jesus was the promised anointed Messiah (Christ) to remove the sin of the world, and to provide the way for man to become His Father's adopted child.

He demonstrated without deviation the commitment to live a life loving your neighbor as yourself, and putting His father's commandments and will above anything or anyone else first, especially self. Because of the lack of knowledge of His chosen people, He was brutally beaten and crucified by the occupying Roman soldiers. All this happened without Him offering one word in His defense, nor did He complain as He willingly in consonance with His mission poured out his life-giving blood, thus establishing the only way by which man could reunite with our Father. Jesus therein matured in complete excellence the perfect intimate relationship for time everlasting, satisfying his Father and fulfilling His mission to provide us a perfect example as to what we must become before being approved by God to enter into His predicted glorious eternity. Throughout His ministry while living in His mortal body, Jesus suffered persecution from His religious brothers, but never any physical ailments common to man until allowing Himself to be scourged prior to his crucifixion.

By praying and meditating on His words I want to emphasize what God has revealed to me. When King James had his many scholars translating (not interpreting) God's language, ancient Hebrew into English, there were some words or phrases for which they had no English word or words that could be used. In those cases they would assume something and would insert it into the text but would italicize it. One such verse is John 12:32, where Jesus is quoted as saying before His crucifixion: "If I be lifted up from the earth, (meaning lifted up on the cross) I will draw all *"men"* (note, men is italicized) unto me." It is obvious that "all" men have not been drawn to Him. But as God revealed to me, "something" that was drawn unto Him was the sum total of all sin in this world: past, present, and future as He was made sin. (Note, not in the likeness of.) He then took this sin along with all sorrows (illnesses) and pain and delivered them in the lap of Satan, who abides in the depth of the earth (hell) and while there took away the keys of death and hell from him.

This has left our adversary Satan without power except that which man allows him to have. Jesus thus fulfilled the first stage of what John the Baptist referenced when Jesus appeared to him to be baptized: "Behold the lamb of God, which taketh away the sin of the world." The second and final stage is after Jesus established God's Kingdom on earth, and Satan is loosed for a season and he gathers those souls that do not conform with Jesus, but want to retain their independent egoism, and they try to make war with Jesus. Instead, these souls are captured and sentenced by God during the great white throne judgment to eternal torment in the lake of fire. This completes the mission of ridding the world of sin.

This type of translation deviation in John 12:32 is very rare and cannot establish that the scriptures contain any errors, but amplify the reason it is necessary to study the word, and not just read the letters of the scripture. The mysteries of the cross are divinely revealed only to those who diligently seek truth. It is true that every man, male or female, who has received Jesus as the son of God, their Redeemer and Savior, has been drawn unto Him by the Cross, but there are those among us who deny that Jesus is Lord.

*   *   *

The above four paradigms have one common denominator, and that is our everlasting, all- powerful and loving Father mandates His children be committed to Him and obedient to His every word, and although we are to love one another as ourselves, we must love everyone and everything, but love them less than we do Him, even our own life. Now since all sin has been removed, this is only one primary objective of our Lord Jesus. The second purpose is recorded in the first epistle of John 3:8, which states, "For this purpose the son of God was manifested, that he might destroy the works of the devil."

There will be countless people inhabiting the earth as Jesus begins His reign as King for the Millennial Age, and time is needed to accomplish all in God's master plan for man and earth. This explains the thousand-year millennial age. It is written in God's word but not clearly defined. In fact His word clearly states that the description of this time should be sealed until the end of days is upon us (Daniel 12:9). This has influenced some religious groups, churches, and many individuals to think it is not intended that men should even consider the signs of the season, which Jesus pointed out in Matthew 24.

I highly recommend you read this very carefully because I believe we are about to experience this glorious time. Relating rightly with the written Word of our Lord is a very important matter and cannot be over-emphasized. The writings of the godly men influenced by the Holy Spirit were first penned in the ancient Hebrew language. Between the third and second centuries before the birth of Christ, all scripture that had been written was translated into the international language of Greece. This is known as the Septuagint. Later writings were also translated into the Greek language. This does not negate the fact that much of the original Hebrew script does not now exist. For example, the Dead Sea scrolls, which are archived along with many other writings, contain writings from every book of the Old Testament except the Book of Ruth. The Greek language is idiomatic in that they have so many different words having distinct and separate meanings that, when translated into English, are the same word. This contributes to some confusion among believers that do not study the word.

An example is in John 20: 5, 8 regarding the word *saw*. In verse 5 the Greek word is *Blepo*, meaning *to behold or look at*. In verse 8, the same word *saw* in Greek is *Eldos,* meaning *to perceive and comprehend*. Studying and understanding the word is necessary for faith- building. The present world happenings indicate we are now there, the end of days; but how long before the rapture, or beginning of the seven-year tribulation period, is an unknown mystery. By His written word, we are to be vigilant and prepared for His visitation.

It is imperative by our seeking His righteousness that by His Grace He removes the veil from the windows of our mind so that we can apprehend and comprehend the purity of the true knowledge of God and Jesus. Concerning the thousand year reign of our Lord as "King of Kings and Lord of Lords," as He literally and physically establishes His everlasting Heavenly Kingdom on this earth, what part might we be called on to serve Him while He rules the nations and subjects of this Kingdom? His church empowered one world government, not the one that will be established by the predicted antichrist. Read Revelation 20:6 very carefully. During this time that we have before the rapture, and the return of Jesus, "The Day of The Lord," when that day is manifest, much is being preached, taught by pastors, Bible teachers, and written by various authors, but is there anything of substance not being taught?

I acknowledge this inspired me to search God's Word. It is about this critical and glorious time in the history of man's total and complete redemption that I write. The most important issues: know who we are, and who our adversary really is. For if we know him and his nature, we, with the protective guidance of Jesus, have the advantage.

The scripture is not the fables of man but are the writings of men of God influenced by God's Holy Spirit, the inerrant uncompromising Word. They were all descendants of Israel, and their law prohibited them from intermarriage or even fraternizing with anyone not of their pure lineage. The exception to this was the apostle Paul, originally Saul of Tarsus, when he was miraculously transformed from earthly carnality to heavenly spiritual reality to preach the gospel to the Gentiles. Recognize that the holy men of God who penned what they were influenced to write, had no knowledge of this difference as they wrote the words that some scripture relates only to the Jew who has refused to accept Jesus as their Messiah, while other scripture relates to all the born-again believers, including Gentiles that have received the Holy Spirit, and represent the true church built by Jesus. Examples are 1 Thessalonians 1: 9-10, and 1 Thessalonians 3:14-16 acknowledging that the orthodox Jew denying that Jesus was their Messiah will have to endure the seven-year tribulation. Yet, a remnant will be saved. His church that He promised to build, consisting of both Jew and Gentile, will escape by rapture the wrath to come. (1 Thessalonians 1:10). In Matthew 24, Jesus warns us to be diligent, not to be deceived, or as written in Ephesians 4:14, "tossed to and fro, and carried about with every wind of doctrine." The Millennial Age to come has a definite purpose and goal in God's overall plan. There is only one plan and it will come to pass. That plan is revealed through the study of His word.

To all persons who have been born again, regardless of nationality, culture, religious affiliations, or intellectual training: While traversing this age, they will become subjects of His Kingdom, along with those who survive the terrible tribulation to come. In addition to having received a new spirit, there is one more thing that has to be embellished before man can enter into his final destination, God's perfected eternity. It is attaining full spiritual maturity with the glorious excellencies of the knowledge of God and Jesus. It is the final stage of our salvation, our sanctification, and the fullness of God in every man, being completed to be an image of His likeness, character, and nature becoming one in spirit with God and Jesus and with one another.

My Personal Relationship with the Lord

A helpful hint from me personally, based upon my meditating and listening for His direction via His Holy Spirit, is to first of all list prayers and consider one basic truth. God's plan is to re-unite man with Him by there being an intimate relationship re-established, and to destroy all the works of Satan the devil.

It is most important to emphasize that the Bible scripture is a very personal and intimate letter from our Heavenly Father. It is His inerrant, uncompromising and loving word to me and you, and must be apprehended by the renewed and refreshed spirit of our minds to capture and retain the truth of His message. While studying His word, I sometimes change the personal pronouns to the first person—me, I, my, and mine—instead of the second or third person—you, yours, our, us, they, theirs, them and those. In this way I put myself into the text of the message and feel closer to my Abba Father, God. For an example: Romans 8:29 originally states: "For those whom He foreknew of whom He was aware and loved beforehand. He also destined from the beginning...to be molded into the image of His Son [and share inwardly His likeness], that he might become the firstborn among many brethren" (Amplified Bible). I'll now read that verse with first-person pronouns interjected: "Because He has known and loved me beforehand, He also destined from the very beginning that I be molded into the image of His Son and share inwardly His likeness so that I, (by choice and obedience) shall become His servant and thus become a victor (overcomer) over evil among my fellow man." Remember, you are reading a personal and intimate letter from your loving Father. The Bible is so majestically designed and expressly reveals His nature for all that have eyes to see, and have ears to hear.

Jesus said, "Take heed that no man deceive you," so with that in mind, search the scriptures and ask the Holy Spirit to either confirm the truth or expose an error in this exciting and challenging saga. It is interesting to note that the word "if" is used 1,595 times in 1,420 verses, and the word "then," meaning afterword or next, is used 2,168 times in 2,115 verses. Each time these two words are used, they denote that some action needs to be taken by man and will require that I exercise my free choice. Therefore, it requires more than just reading the letter of the word.

Some Important Bible References

Revelation 21:7

"If I am an overcomer, then I shall inherit all things, and Jesus will be my God and I shall be His son."

2 Corinthians 13:5

This is the only scripture that authorizes me to judge. I must examine, test and evaluate myself to judge whether I am holding to faith expecting and producing acceptable fruit for the Kingdom and pleasing God. At the same time I must humbly recognize that the Spirit of Jesus is within me, or am I weak or even void of faith relying on God to do everything for me?

Matthew 7:21

First know that Heaven is the seat of all God's government, judgment, and origin of commands and declarations that created all. One other note is Heaven was never, and is not now, meant to be the permanent habitat for man. That has always been and is today the purpose of earth. Unfortunately, God's adversary has been able to infiltrate into the body of believers with deceitful doctrine. It is imperative that you and I not be deceived by any scripture other than that influenced by God's Holy Spirit, who is the only source of true interpretation (2 Peter 1:20). Yet I must not judge others, but I am to continually search the Scripture for His truths.

Revelation 2:26-27; and 3:21

If I am an overcomer and have been obedient without wavering, faithfully doing what is pleasing to God, He will grant me (or allow me) to sit with him on His throne in the same manner that He did on the throne of His Father. He may allow me the privilege to assist Him in His mission being a priest of God to accomplish the purpose of the Millennial Age. This bears witness to the absolute righteousness of His rule over His Kingdom for ages upon ages. His authority is absolute and established and according to 2 Timothy 4:8: "If I am declared an over- comer, to receive a crown of righteousness for being faithful and obedient to the good works of Jesus, I may be assigned a definite responsibility serving the King. Think of the scepter not as a weapon, or a tool for punishment, it is spiritually similar to 'the rod of Moses', it being the Holy Spirit's release point of power."

Psalm 8:5-6

"For thou hast made him a little lower than the angels, and hast crowned him with glory and honor....Thou made him to have dominion over the works of thy hands; thou hast put all [things] under his feet" (King James Version).

The previous verse starts out with the question, "What is man?" According to 1 Corinthians 3:6, and 2 Corinthians 6:1, we are to be co-workers or co-laborers with Jesus, and have all dominion over all the earth. This is really provocative, for even the angels in God's Heavenly Kingdom did not know what God was doing. God's anointed cherub was one of them; and when he heard the blessing given to Adam, jealousy gripped him, and he then put into action his diabolic scheme to steal that blessing, and he succeeded. I believe it was the proverbial "straw that broke the camel's back" that sealed his doom and a patient, loving, and forgiving God had him, and all power of evil, expelled from His Kingdom in Heaven and cast into the earth. It matters not when but that he was expelled and became the god of this world until Jesus stripped him of all power and retrieved the blessing given to man.

Genesis 3:23-24

After the success of God's renegade angel to steal God's Blessing, God removed Adam and Eve from the Garden of Eden. He also blocked the entrance to the garden so they could not re-enter it. Some have considered this a punishment and the wrath of God; but it was in truth His compassionate love to keep them from taking of the fruit of the tree of life. By their disobedience of God, they had allowed Satan the right and means to afflict them with all or any of the contaminations of sin. Had they eaten the fruit from the tree of life, they would have never died and would never have had to live a living hell afflicted with perpetual disease or affliction.

Just think, some time in our future we will have the opportunity to meet Adam and Eve in the millennium Kingdom to come, if not before.

Revelation 21:7

"All that overcomes evil will inherit all things and be my son!"

Read it as a personal prophecy concerning you. If or when we are victorious, then we shall inherit all these things; and Jesus will be our God, and we will be His servant and co-worker throughout the Millennial Age of preparation. There is yet a lot we must learn and understand and much to do. Pray that all blinded minds that are prevalent today be cleared so as to enable all men to understand God's truths in the scripture. All those who inherit rewards will have to work assisting Jesus during His reign in the Millennial Age by counseling and teaching with compassionate love to manifest the fullness of God in every soul before the final judgment day, and before entering into God's perfected eternity. God's master plan is to complete in every soul the salvation afforded through the blood of Jesus to every man before entering into the final age of eternity. This mandates that the God/man relationship be restored to the intimacy that existed between God and Adam in the beginning of the age.

*   *   *

I write all this to inform you to believe Jesus and be diligent, for your salvation is nigh, and all they that think they are saved, unless they be born of the spirit, born again, and have relinquished all selfness to Jesus our Lord, they are in for a tragic surprise. It is not too late. Just open your heart to the Holy Spirit to receive God's blessing, and He will do the rest.

CHAPTER 13

The Hope of All Glory

The purpose of man, the purpose of trials through life, are the finishing goal which is the will of God for every man, for His desire is that none should perish. Through attaining full knowledge and understanding of our Lord Jesus, we fervently work toward, and reach our destiny the hope of Glory. Hebrews 10:23 states: "Let us hold fast the confession of our hope without wavering, for He who promised is faithful."

I know now after these many years that every word of prophecy or instruction, or commandment printed in the Bible, is inerrant, and those spoken by Jesus or by God were quoted righteously by the forty holy men who wrote the absolute truths of the scriptures. I am looking forward to partake of all God's blessed promises for time everlasting, saying goodbye to this evil world, and saying hello to God and Jesus in His Glorious Eternity. But first we will serve our Lord Jesus as his servant and priest as we partake of the duties associated with the Millennial Age to bring to all men the fullness of the knowledge of God and Jesus, and realize the closeness and love of our real Father.

Just picture in your mind a world of harmony and beauty that is ineffable, a world where there is no sickness or pain, where there are no doctors, no nurses, no hospitals, no pharmacies and drugs, no funeral homes, no deaths, no cemeteries or head stones. There will be nothing to pollute or contaminate earthly environments. It is a promised place without time, so you won't get old and lose your sight, hearing, or hair, or become senile and ever-dependent on others for assistance.

There will be no churches, for we will worship our Spirit Father and Jesus face-to-face. We will be one with Him and with each other with no more emotions influencing any disorder or discord over such things as color of skin, origin of birth, slant of eyes, color or length of hair, and manner of dress, as we will experience among us perfect harmony and love. All manner of discord will be replaced with the total love of God within each of us. The first and second commandments will be fulfilled, and we will be one with God and love Him with our entire heart, soul, and mind. We will lover our neighbors as ourselves, and love each other as Jesus loves us.

The faithful and anointed apostle Peter wrote in his first epistle, the first chapter: "We should continually bless, and give all praise to our heavenly father, the father of our lord Jesus the Christ, for it is by His abundant grace, and great mercy that we have been Spirit born. Born again from above by God's Holy Spirit, because He had raised our Jesus from the dead. It is because of this we can now live with great expectation, a lively hope that we have a priceless inheritance incorruptible and undefiled and will never, no, never fade away." This exceedingly great and wondrous prize is the hope of all Glory, which should be everyone's goal with purpose for our earthly life, and is kept in heaven, pure and without any corruption, to be given all God's children at the end of this age and the beginning of eternity, home at last.

There is a parable that reveals a mystery concerning this time and place, the beginning of God's final age of eternity. You will recognize it as the first miracle performed by Jesus: turning water into wine. The occasion was a time of joy, a wedding feast. Mary the mother of Jesus was in attendance. When the host, the bridegroom, had run out of wine, Mary summoned Jesus and told him the problem. He did not address her as "mom" or "mother." He said, "Woman, what does this have to do with me?" She did not answer Him but, addressing servants, said, "Do exactly as he demands."

There were six large water urns, each capable of containing thirty gallons of fluid. Jesus commanded the servants to fill each urn with water (180 gallons). He then directed one servant to draw a cup of

106

the fluid and take it to the "feast master." After the feast master partook of the fluid, he summoned the bridegroom, whom he complemented for saving the best wine till last!

I will now reveal what has been given me, a more informative saga. It is a message concealed within this parable. In it, there are no explicitly identifiable characters, so I will identify them for you:

- The feast master is our Father, the most High and mighty God.
- The bridegroom is Jesus.
- The bride is His Church.

The bottom line is, He has saved the best for last, for all His church in the age to come. God has sealed the time and true description of what we will inherit. This is evident in three places in scripture:

- First in Daniel 12:6-8
- Second in 2 Corinthians 12:2-4
- Third in Revelation 10:1-4

And the writers were instructed that the knowledge shown them was to be sealed until the end of days.

All I know is that it will be exceedingly wondrous. Yet there are two things of which we should be knowledgeable and diligently aware. If not, we may be snared into false doctrine, for today the airwaves and church pulpits are bursting with man's limited commentaries, analyses, and interpretations concerning this age in which we live. First we must learn the truth of ourselves.

First, know that we possess all God's grace-given gifts from our Father and the wisdom to use and apply them continually. We have inherently received the power of the Holy Ghost abiding within us. Second, remember that we must recognize our calling, for we have all been called to a particular function within the body of Christ, then given ample efficiency to accomplish our mission in His church wherein by the love and faith we have for our Lord Jesus, and all Saints. Know that our communication and sharing of our faith, which is our personal gift, may become effectual by our acknowledging of every good thing within us in Christ Jesus. This gift we must acknowledge and not be reluctant to expound it to the world. We must not be ashamed of our testimony (Ephesians 1:3; Philemon 6; and 2 Timothy 2:8). Finally, we must always keep in mind that all He has promised and done for us brings us eventually to harvest.

The Best Is Yet to Come!

Let me now expound on the Hope of All Glory. This earth has seen the life of man for about six thousand years. Ignoring the flood during Noah's time, there have been billions of living souls traversing the maze of life and never finding what it is all about. Yet there was and still is a grand and holy purpose that few have ever found.

Recognize that God is a Spirit. He made man in His image and after His likeness. We are therefore primarily spirits living in a mortal body; but, due to the contamination and corruption of sin, we must be purified. Think of the process to purify precious metals from all impurity. Let us consider silver: The unrefined ore is placed in a large ladle, then placed in a large furnace. The ore is liquefied by being exposed to extreme heat. After it is liquefied it is removed from the furnace, and the impurities that have risen to the top are skimmed off the liquefied ore. This process is repeated seven times before the product is purified from all impurities. The end product is pure silver.

Now, in comparison, our journey through life is a spiritual experience made up of multiple events, both spiritual and physical; and because of sin we are impure. But all events contribute to our purification in order that we partake of the Hope of All Glory with our Heavenly father in a purified heavens and earth for eternity. This will be done during the Millennial Age with Jesus as He rules as King.

It is our Father's will for His absolute blessing for His children. I remind you to keep your attention on Jesus, for he is a Perfect Paradigm.

* * *

The message within this story is there is a purpose in life. It is to earn the approbation of our Heavenly Father, and be accepted and converted into His family. Finally, our goal should be to partake of His will, for we shall inherit a permanent home with Him in His heaven on earth for eternity.

That is our hope of all Glory.

Yes, life with Jesus makes it all worth living.

The Best is Yet to Come

www.ingramcontent.com/pod-product-compliance
Lightning Source LLC
Chambersburg PA
CBHW030419100426
42812CB00028B/3027/J